THE AUTHOR HEIR HANDBOOK

HOW TO MANAGE AN AUTHOR

M.L. RONN

Special thank you to the following people on Patreon who supported this book: BB Dee, Matty Dalrymple, Cariad Eccleston, Stephen Frans, Michael Guishard, Jon Howard, Beth Jackson, S. Chipasula Perry, Lynda Washington, and Etta Welk.

Some links in this book contain affiliate links. If you purchase books and services through these links, I receive a small commission at no cost to you. You are under no obligation to use these links, but thank you if you do!

For more helpful writing tips and advice, subscribe to the Author Level Up YouTube channel: www. youtube.com/authorlevelup.

This book provides an overview of estate planning and managing an author estate as an heir. The contents should not be taken as legal advice or opinion. While every effort has been made to be accurate, this book should not be relied upon as the sole basis of planning an estate. If you need legal advice, contact a lawyer in your country, state, and/province. It is highly recommended that you use this book as a starting point and that you ultimately seek the counsel of a skilled lawyer, financial advisor, and accountant to build an estate plan that works for you and your family.

CONTENTS

MANAGING THE ESTATE: MAKING MONEY

INTRODUCTION

Dear Heir,

If you're reading this book, that means you have inherited (or are going to inherit) an author estate. All or most of the author's books, writings, and other property will belong to you. If you're like many authors' heirs, you have no idea what to do with them.

The author giving this inheritance to you could be a spouse, parent, sibling, child, relative, or close friend. (From now on, I will refer to them as "the author.")

You were probably close to the author, and you know that writing was important to them. You know very well how much time they spent on the writing life—usually in a room alone. They might have even told you what they were working on, and about the struggles they encountered and their successes. But probably, the writing world is still a mystery to you.

Now, as you look at all the pieces of the estate they left behind, you may be feeling lost, overwhelmed, anxious, and helpless. You have been chosen to keep the author's books alive, but you may not feel that you can. You may wish you had paid more attention or asked more questions about what they were doing.

It is now your responsibility to keep the author's publishing business running, keep the money flowing, and—in the case of many author estates— pay the other heirs regularly. It's a lot to handle, but not impossible.

All of this was tough for the author to handle too. Sadly, I don't know very many authors who choose to get their affairs in order while they're alive.

But it is what it is and now you are in charge.

The goal of this book is to make you aware of what is possible. It will point you in the right direction so you can understand how to manage the estate properly.

Believe it or not, you may be able to do more with the author's estate than they ever did in their lifetime.

About Me

My name is M.L. Ronn (Michael La Ronn). At the time of this writing, I am the author of over 70 books of science fiction and fantasy and self-help books for writers. I also host a popular YouTube channel for authors called "Author Level Up" that has nearly 40,000 subscribers. I've spoken at many renowned author conferences, and I built a writing career while working a full-time job in insurance, raising a family, and attending law school classes in the evenings.

I understand the author life because I live it every day.

I decided to learn estate planning because I realized that if I died unexpectedly, I would be leaving a mess for my family. Unless I did something, my books were going to die with me.

I wrote a book on estate planning for authors, and in the process of planning my own estate, I realized just how difficult this process can be, especially for heirs.

(If the author is still alive, I would recommend purchasing my book, **The Author Estate Handbook,** as it is a great conversation starter. Combined with the book you're currently reading, you and the author will be able to get on the same page before they pass away. It will make managing the estate much, much easier.)

Disclaimers

Nothing in this book should be considered financial, tax, or legal advice. For specific help, you need to contact a financial adviser, accountant, or lawyer in your area. This book also assumes that you are finished with probate (or that you didn't need it). It's a good idea to settle the estate or get your estate attorney's permission before you start taking the actions I recommend in this book. Otherwise, you could find yourself in violation of probate laws, and we don't want that!

Take care of the final arrangements, get the estate settled, and get yourself okay with your attorney and the court. Take all the time you need to grieve and get yourself in a position to manage the estate. Then, take the steps in this book.

While some urgent things need attention after the author passes, nothing is more important than taking care of pending legal matters (and yourself).

Also, if you make a mistake at any point in managing the estate, be kind to yourself. There are very few manuals or resources on managing author estates, which is why I wrote this book. If you can avoid the biggest mistakes that I discuss in this book, almost everything else is fixable. You're on a journey and you won't always get it right at first. But you'll get better with time.

As I said, be kind to yourself.

This Book is in Plain English

I want to make sure that you understand that I understand that you may not know very much about publishing, self-publishing, or running an author business. That's why I kept this book concise.

I also will never assume that you understand what a term means. The publishing industry is full of jargon, and I will define terms frequently in this book.

Now that we've gotten the basics out of the way, let's get started.

FIRST ORDER OF BUSINESS

First, let's define "estate." According to the **Oxford English Dictionary**, it is "all the money and property owned by a particular person, especially at death."

An author's estate does not exist until they die—thus why they must plan for its eventual existence. Such a plan is called an estate plan. In an estate plan, the author must plan for how money and property (also known as "assets") will be distributed after their death. The part of an author's estate that contains the copyrights is sometimes called a literary estate.

The "executor" (also "executrix" or "personal representative") is the person the author designates to run the estate, settle the author's affairs, and handle the money, usually designated in a will. A court must appoint an executor. If you're reading this, those responsibilities have probably fallen upon you.

"Heirs" (also known as "beneficiaries") are the people the author designates to receive (or benefit from) the assets. Heirs are usually spouses, children, or grandchildren, but not always. In addition to being an executor, you are probably also an heir, and you may be responsible for sharing the author's assets with other heirs.

Here's the key difference between the estates of a typical person and an author.

In a typical person's estate, the income stops when a person dies. Their assets are distributed and their estates are settled in court via probate or through a trust. When the judge bangs the gavel, everyone moves on. The author, however, has created an estate where the heirs don't have that luxury. The traditional parts of the author's estate will be settled like everyone else's, but the author part of the estate will be an ongoing responsibility. This is because the author's books will continue to generate income, and, in many countries, will do so for 70 years after the author's death. Even after that, the estate can still profit from the author's work!

The uniqueness of the author estate requires the executor to carry out duties on an ongoing basis, far longer than a typical executor ever would. You will carry this responsibility at least until the end of your life or until you can no longer do so. If your successor is a child (young or old), this responsibility could last for their entire life too.

This is why I hope that the author was extremely organized.

In writing this book and **The Author Estate Handbook**, one of my biggest challenges was finding good advice that was appropriate for authors. Some estate planning advice that works for typical people does not work for authors. For example, it's difficult to find an attorney who understands copyright and writing businesses—my personal experience was that most of the attorneys I consulted had no idea how to handle my books. My first will was handled poorly and would have made it impossible for my wife to conduct any affairs after my death. All but one of the attorneys I met with counseled me on how to avoid things that most people never think of after death, like writing down passwords, banks freezing accounts, and preventing access to much-needed funds. And even then, I had to ask these questions.

My point is that there is a serious lack of information on author estate planning, and especially author estate management. You will have this working against you until more authors die and more estates exist for authors who mastered the new world of publishing we are currently in.

In many ways, you are a pioneer. I'm not exaggerating when I say that if you find a way to become successful in managing the author's estate, you will make it possible for many other families to do the same.

The Three Stages of Estate Planning

. . .

There are three stages to estate planning, and
they are:

- **Planning**. The author decides how they
  want their estate to be handled. This is
  when they draft wills, trusts, and other
  estate planning documents.
- **Organization**. The author gets their affairs
  in order and documents what you need to
  know about taking over the publishing
  business when they're gone.
- **Management**. The author passes away and
  you take over.

The Management stage can be broken into three
stages:

- **Securing the Estate**. You gather all the
  pieces of the estate and figure out what
  you have.

- **Organizing the Estate**. You organize everything for your benefit so that you can run the estate efficiently.
- **Managing the Estate**. You start managing the estate and reaping the benefits of the author's work.

There is a lot we have to do before we can get to the "Managing the Estate" part of estate management. This book will help you get there as quickly and efficiently as possible.

YOU'VE INHERITED A SMALL BUSINESS

The first concept for you to understand is that by inheriting an author's books, you are inheriting a small business.

This might sound strange, especially if the author didn't treat their books like a business. Many authors don't like to do that because of preconceived notions about art and business, but we have to live in reality.

A business has expenses and income, and it strives to earn a profit.

Before the author published their books, they probably hired editors and cover designers. Those are expenses.

Authors also pay for websites and advertising, which are also expenses.

When the author published their books, those books earned income.

At tax time, the author had to pay taxes on profits made from their books.

So, make no mistake: whether the author treated their efforts like a business or not, you are inheriting a business. If you want to manage the estate correctly, you must treat it as a small business.

Perhaps you already have experience running a business. If you do, then you have an advantage. However, if the thought of running a business worries you, then you need to educate yourself on business basics. It's not hard, but it requires knowledge, because you can make some big mistakes if you're not careful.

· · ·

What Was the Author's Business Entity?

For tax purposes, every author has to have a legal business entity for their publishing business. You can find this by looking at the author's tax returns.

Many authors are sole proprietors (or sole traders in the UK). This means that there is no legal separation between the author and the business.

Other options include a corporation or a limited liability company.

The most important thing you can do is consult with an accountant and an attorney to determine how you will handle taxes moving forward. Everyone's situation will be different, so I can't give you any advice other than to seek professional assistance. As an heir, you have your own life, wealth, passions, and possibly other business obligations that you will have to merge with the author's publishing business, and it will require a smart tax and legal strategy.

However, do remember that most accountants and attorneys do not work with creative estates, so you've got that working against you. If you already have a professional you're used to working with and prefer not to change them, at least seek second opinions from someone who understands author or creative estates. Otherwise, you could make a mistake to your detriment. Never assume that just because something works for a regular person that it will work for an author estate. You've been warned.

It's Not Just Book Income You Have to Worry About

When I talk to people about author estates, they often have a romantic image in their heads. They don't think they have to do anything. They expect to relax and pursue their own passions while automatic book income hits their bank account every month, with very little effort on their part. What a dream!

Unfortunately, that is not what you're inheriting.

Taking over a book business is a lot of work. You can sit back and take the money if you want, but you'll find that the money will reduce to almost nothing over time.

A better way to think about a book business is like inheriting a garden. It takes a lot of effort to get a garden going, but it takes just as much effort to maintain it too. If you don't keep up with the garden, everything in it will eventually die.

First, the author's business will have expenses that you will need to maintain. For example, you will be responsible for maintaining the author's website so that readers can find the author's books. That requires time and money.

You will also have to refresh the author's books from time to time with new covers and new book descriptions because tastes change and you'll need to keep the author relevant. Longer term, you will need to find ways to introduce the author's books to new generations of readers.

To illustrate this, think about an author estate in the year 2000. Back then, paperbacks were the predominant book format. E-books didn't truly exist and audiobooks were on cassettes. If you were running an estate back then, a publisher would have handled everything for you. It was a very different world.

Fast forward to 2007 and the advent of the Kindle. As the executor, you would have noticed some radical changes:

- Readers were increasingly buying their books online, especially on Amazon.
- The internet transformed society, democratizing book discovery and making it easier for readers to find more books than they ever could before the advent of the internet.
- The Kindle led to an explosion of demand for e-books.
- The rise of smartphones, podcasting, and faster mobile internet connections made it possible for audiobook MP3s to replace audiobook cassettes in popularity.

- Authors were becoming more frustrated with traditional publishers, finding ways to get out of their original publishing contracts so that they could self-publish their books and exercise more control.

See how quickly the industry changes? That's just seven years, which is not very much time. If you were a savvy executor in charge of the estate in 2007, you would have noticed these trade winds and wanted to capitalize on them. Otherwise, the estate would have been left behind (as many were).

The same will be true seven years from whenever you are reading this.

Nothing in the publishing industry stays still. We haven't even started talking about how book genres change over time. For example, what romance readers read in 2000 is drastically different from what they're reading in 2022.

If you still think you're going to sit back and wait for the money to flow to you, you're dooming the estate. You'll be able to get by for a few years without doing very much, but if you want to continue earning income from the estate (and growing it), you will need to keep up and evolve with the industry. That requires work on your part, which is why I hope the author prepared you for it.

If this chapter overwhelmed you, remember that you've inherited a business, so you can hire help. You might even be able to hire some of the same people who helped the author. Fortunately, you have many options at your disposal, and we'll discuss them later in the book.

Never forget that you are in charge of a publishing business. That business may not be producing any new books, but the books you have can be very lucrative.

Review The Income Sources

. . .

Take some time to review the author's last two years' worth of tax documents. That will tell you where the money is coming from.

One important thing to understand about a publishing business in today's digital age is that it consists of many, many streams of income.

Amazon is one stream of income. Apple is another. The average author has dozens of income streams. They may not necessarily report them all to the government. (Though they should!)

Many of the income streams start small. Very small. They might only be a few dollars a year. Others might be gigantic. But expect there to be a lot of income streams because the author with the most income streams wins.

Let me give you an example of all the income streams I currently have in my publishing business.

- I sell e-books at fifty different retailers. Each retailer is a stream of income.
- I sell paperbacks at three retailers, with the ability to sell to bookstores and libraries.

- I sell audiobooks.
- I sell books directly on my website.
- I sell online courses.
- I promote products and services I recommend, and I receive compensation when people buy those products (known as affiliate income).
- I am a YouTuber and my videos are monetized.
- I do paid speaking events.
- I consult with publishing businesses for a fee.
- I have a Patreon community where my biggest fans support me each month.
- I sell merchandise in the theme of my books and brand.
- I sell short stories and poetry to literary magazines.

That's just scratching the surface of all my income streams. You may have just as many or more to manage in the estate.

Count those income streams! Eventually, you will want to look for ways to add streams to the business.

Review

You have inherited a small business. Never forget that.

Determine your tax and legal strategy moving forward.

Count the income streams coming into the business.

If you start with these simple steps, you'll put yourself in a better position to manage the estate properly.

A QUICK INTRODUCTION TO COPYRIGHT

The next thing you must understand is copyright because that's how authors make their money.

You may have heard the term "copyright" but didn't know what it meant.

According to **Merriam Webster**, copyright is "the exclusive legal right to reproduce, publish, sell, or distribute the matter and form of something (such as a literary, musical, or artistic work)."

Copyright is a form of "intellectual property." You've probably heard of real property (as in real estate) and personal property (like jewelry and other valuables), but intellectual property is a third and often overlooked type of property. According to **Merriam Webster**, intellectual property is "property (such as an idea, invention, or process) that derives from the work of the mind or intellect."

When an author writes a book, they've just created a piece of intellectual property, even if they don't publish it. Copyright protection begins the moment the author types the words on the page.

In some countries like the United States, authors are encouraged to "register" their copyrights with the Copyright Office. The main reason to do this is that you must register a work to sue someone for "infringing" on it. When someone infringes on a copyright, it means they are using the work or making money from it without the author's permission. For example, if someone pirates the author's novel by making it available for download on an illicit website, that's copyright infringement. If the author wants to take that person to court, they will have to register the work with the government first. While this is true in the United States, it is not necessarily true in other countries.

Copyright is often overlooked because it is "intangible," meaning it can't be touched. When you die, most of your property is tangible. You can see and touch a house or personal belongings. A book manuscript, while it may have a paperback edition, isn't tangible. This is why people forget that it has value. Many assume that it does not, which is unfortunate.

But as you know, the author makes money every time someone buys one of their books, and they can earn this income for their life plus 70 years in many countries.

The best way to think about a copyrighted work is that it is infinitely indivisible. When we refer to a copyrighted work, what we're really referring to is a bundle of works.

If an author publishes a novel, they can publish it in different formats:

- an e-book edition
- a paperback edition
- a hardcover edition
- a large print edition

- an audiobook
- and more.

It is completely up to the author to decide which editions of the book to create. If a book is especially successful, the author may be able to create even more formats:

- a movie
- a television show
- a video game
- a game show
- a board game
- a graphic novel
- and more

The only limit is the author's imagination.

The simplest example of copyright licensing is the **Harry Potter** series by J.K. Rowling. It started as a series of books, but look at all the different products in the Harry Potter franchise now:

- movies
- video games

- clothing
- spinoff books
- a Broadway show
- an amusement park
- a game show
- and many more

Just to reiterate, what could have been just one book series became many different intellectual properties.

And here's where the magic of copyright lies: J.K Rowling didn't sell her copyrights. She "licensed" them. When you sell something, it becomes the property of another person or company, and you never see any more benefits from owning it. When you license it, you only license part of the copyright to someone else, and you keep the rest. The person or company you license the work to usually has an ongoing obligation to pay you proceeds from their success in creating a new version of the work. You can even negotiate the license to return to you at some point in the future. When Rowling licensed the book into new formats, she kept the rights to everything else. This is how she was able to capitalize on the brand, spinning off product after product. All of the products she licensed became streams of income that flowed back to her, which allowed her to create even more products. Now she's richer than the British crown!

That's the beauty of copyright when done properly: you license it, not sell it. If you remember that copyright is an infinite bundle of rights, then anything is possible!

In our case, one book can become many things, and each of those things can become a stream of income for the author (and the author's estate).

Every book is different and has a different nature. A lot depends on timing. For example, the author might write a book about a topic that isn't popular when they publish it, but the topic could grow in popularity over the next decade, and suddenly, many people want to read books about it.

A lot also depends on the nature of the work. Some books lend themselves better to movies than others, for example. I know an author whose short story was optioned for a movie, but Hollywood won't touch any of their novels!

The key is to understand the following:

- The author's works have the potential to be extremely valuable even though they may not look like it. Never underestimate a book's potential.
- Copyright is an infinite bundle of rights. Your only limit of what you can do with the author's work is your imagination.
- The author planted the seeds, and the author couldn't have known how many of them would grow. Your job is to be the gardener—to cultivate the potential of the works and harvest the rewards of the author's hard work.

All of this may sound silly over, say, a little novel the author wrote in a weekend and didn't think twice about, but if there's one thing you should internalize, it's to never take anything for granted.

The author never knew when opportunity would strike. You won't either. As the saying goes, fortune favors the prepared mind. When you understand copyright, you can start spotting opportunities to make money with the author's work.

I've included a resource guide in the appendix that will help you get up to speed with more key copyright concepts you'll need to understand.

A QUICK INTRODUCTION TO PUBLISHING

Now that you understand the basics of copyright, let's talk about how authors publish their books. This is a simple overview of the two publishing styles that the author would have used.

A Primer on Traditional Publishing

Until 2007, the most common (and viable) way to publish a book was through a publisher. This is called "traditional" publishing. A traditional publisher could be a large publishing conglomeration like Penguin Random House, HarperCollins, or Macmillan, or it could be a mid-sized publishing house like Tor, or it could be a "small press," which is a publishing house with a small staff that publishes a handful of titles per year.

Regardless of how the author traditionally published, they had to pitch their idea to a literary agent or a publisher. If the manuscript was a work of fiction, the author had to send a "synopsis" of the novel, which is a short pitch on what the novel is about. If the manuscript was a work of nonfiction, the author had to send an outline of the book. If the publisher liked the idea, then they would offer a publishing contract.

A publishing contract is between the author and the publisher, and in plain English, the author usually licenses their copyright to the publisher. In practice, it's not that simple.

Traditional publishing contracts have a reputation for being draconian. In any copyright negotiation, the author should limit the formats being licensed. For example, it makes no sense to license an audiobook edition to a publisher who doesn't plan on creating an audiobook edition! However, because big publishers have all the leverage in negotiations, that's exactly what happens. Not only do they take the e-book, paperback, and audiobook rights, they will take as many rights to the book as possible, including grabs at the author's next books too. Some contracts may even take the copyright altogether—commonly called "life of copyright contracts." If the author doesn't like it, tough luck.

I hope you can see now why this is bad. Yet, traditional publishers are frequently romanticized by people who don't know any better.

Traditional publishers take on all the risk, so they pay the author a small percentage of sales. They usually pay quarterly or annually. In many cases, the author's literary agent may be responsible for sending payment, which in my opinion is an invitation for embezzlement. (The literary agent also receives a percentage of every book sale).

Another wrinkle: if the author signed a traditional publishing contract, they received an "advance," which is an advance payment against future income. If the book doesn't sell well, it may not "earn out" its advance, which means that the publisher won't owe any payments to the author until it does.

Also, what happens if the publisher does a terrible job with the book? What if they don't promote it? The author is stuck because the publisher holds the rights and has the final say.

There are myriad other issues with traditional publishing—too many to cover in this short book.

If the author traditionally published any books, your first order of business needs to be finding the publishing contracts. The contracts will tell you what the author licensed (or sold), what the payment terms are, and any limitations the author (and you) may be under.

Most importantly, you will want to make sure you notify the publisher of the author's death so they can send the royalties to you.

If the contract is especially bad, you may wish to figure out a way to escape the contract so you can get the rights back. In the United States, you can do this under the principle of copyright termination. The resources in the appendix will help you explore this further.

A Primer on Self-publishing

With the advent of the Kindle in 2007, authors were empowered to self-publish their work and cut out traditional publishers. Self-publishing isn't new, but historically, you had to pay a lot of money to a company that would make shoddy-quality books, and it wasn't a serious route to building a publishing career. Self-publishing carried a nasty stigma for a long time, something that people still associate with it today, but self-publishing doesn't deserve bad press anymore. A self-published author today is a completely different author than someone who did it in the 1990s or early 2000s.

Now authors can create online accounts at various book retailers, publish their books, and reach readers directly. As a result, many authors make a substantial income from their books.

The savviest of these authors treat their publishing operations like a business. They hire professional editors and cover designers, and they perform all the same functions that a traditional publisher would. They make it so that you can't tell the difference between their book and a traditionally-published one. Many authors are making more money than they ever could have on the traditional side, and readers have shown that they don't care who publishes a book so long as it is good. Quality is everything.

Traditional publishers only pay a small percentage of each book sale; the payments from self-publishing are much higher because there's no intermediary.

For e-books, self-published writers make anywhere from 60 to 70 percent from each e-book sale (with some minor exceptions from retailer to retailer). An e-book priced at $4.99 will net anywhere from $2.99 to $3.50, with the rest going to the retailer.

For paperbacks, the margins are smaller because the author has to pay for printing costs. However, self-publishers use "print on-demand" services like KDP

Print or IngramSpark, so the author only pays printing costs when the book is sold, and the cost is subtracted from the sale. You don't have to worry about inventory or stacks of books in your garage. For a typical paperback priced at $14.99, the author might take home between $5 and $6.

For audiobooks, the pricing is a little more complicated. Audible is the biggest audiobook retailer, and they had a near monopoly on the market for many years, though there have been competitors like Spotify challenging them recently. At the time of this writing, audiobooks on Audible sell between $7.49 and $24.99. Audible determines the price of an audiobook based on its length. It determines the sales commission based on whether the book is exclusive to Audible. Let's take an audiobook priced at $7.49. If the author makes a title exclusive to Audible, their net sale could be anywhere from $1.50 to $2.99. If the author makes a title non-exclusive to Audible (meaning they sell it at other audiobook retailers), the net sale cuts in half to $0.75 to $1.50. Audible pricing is complex.

Other audiobook retailers are much more reasonable and give you a fairer percentage of the sale.

As far as book production, the author is in charge. They must learn how to create a book cover, format a book for e-book and print, and take on other day-to-day tasks that traditional publishers historically handled. This can be overwhelming, but most authors hire freelancers (people who offer their services to the public for a fee) to help with these tasks. In your case, the author probably hired cover designers and editors.

If the author self-published any titles, your first order of business should be to figure out which book retailers they used. Most authors use several online accounts to publish, and it's more lucrative to publish directly with a retailer. This means that they may have individual accounts with Amazon, Apple, Barnes & Noble, and so on. While this was certainly a best practice for the author, it's not so much for you because you'll have a lot of dashboards to manage!

. . .

Recap

In the self-publishing model, the author is responsible for everything.

In the traditional publishing model, the author is only responsible for marketing. The publisher takes care of the rest. (But as we discussed, that's not necessarily a good thing).

Some authors have a mixture of traditionally and self-published books, and those authors are known as "hybrid authors."

Look at your author's catalog. Which books are traditionally-published and which ones are self-published?

If your author mostly traditionally published their books, your estate will be very contract-oriented. It will be your responsibility to understand the contracts the author signed and how to navigate around any limitations. You will also need to hold the publishers accountable.

If your author mostly self-published their books, your estate will be very hands-on because it will be up to you to continue the work the author started. You'll need to make sure that the books remain available for sale, which is harder than it sounds.

That's your quick primer to the publishing world. Feel free to read this chapter a couple of times—it's okay if you didn't understand it all. There's so much more to learn, but if you understand this chapter on a basic level, you'll have all the knowledge you need to get started.

SECURING THE ESTATE: GATHERING THE PIECES

It's time to start gathering all the pieces of the estate. Take your time and read this section carefully. It will help you make sense of the author's business model, how much intellectual property you have, and how much work will be involved in managing the estate.

DEVICES

Take your time with this chapter and be very thorough.

We need to secure the first critical part of the estate.

First, secure the author's writing computer and any devices they used to write their books, such as phones and tablets. When I say "secure," I mean make sure that you can access the devices without limitations.

If the author used passwords, I hope you have them. If not, you'll need to find them. If you can't, you'll need to hire a computer technician to see if they can break into the device. This will be expensive and there is no certainty they will succeed, but it's an option of last resort.

It goes without saying that if you can't get access to the author's devices, then managing their estate will be extremely difficult. Not impossible, but way more difficult than it has to be.

Once you secure access to the devices, look through them and figure out the locations of three key files.

Key Files #1: The Manuscripts

These are the book manuscripts. Along with the manuscripts, you will also find the author's research, notes, outlines, character sketches, and other items they used in the creation of the manuscript, which are all valuable to the estate.

First, find the author's writing app. This is the app they used to write all of their books. Go to the settings and figure out where the program saves the manuscripts. If you can find that folder, you will likely find the location of all of the author's manuscripts.

Key Files #2: Final Book Files

Congratulations on finding the manuscripts.

However, anything the author creates in their writing app is not likely to be the final, formatted version of the book. This is because many authors use formatting software to create the interior layouts for their books. (The interior is everything between the front and back covers.)

The main reason authors use formatting software is because without it, creating e-books and paperbacks that meet retailer specifications can be manual and time-consuming. Paperback interiors in particular are almost impossible to format correctly and well unless you really know what you're doing. Many authors avoided paperbacks altogether until dedicated formatting apps came along.

Usually, an author's formatting software is different from their writing app (but not always). Formatting apps took off in popularity around 2017 and many authors are now using them.

Formatting apps include Vellum (for Mac), Atticus (web-based), and even Adobe InDesign. But probably, the author was using Vellum or Atticus. If they were in a pinch and strapped for money, they may have used Microsoft Word.

In any case, when you run a book through a formatting app, it produces a final formatted file that the author can upload to retailers.

Final formatted files have the following extensions: EPUB, MOBI, and PDF. Search for EPUB and MOBI files on the computer and see what you find.

Given what I know about how many authors are operating today, I'm willing to bet that the book manuscripts and the final formatted files will probably be in separate locations. It's annoying for your purposes, but helpful to know.

My final point should be obvious, but I'll say it anyway: any time in the future when you need to make change to a book, you need to update the final formatted file. If the author used a formatting app, you would make the change in the app and use it to create new versions of those files.

What To Do If You Can't Find the Files

Don't panic. It's not the end of the world if you can't find the manuscripts or final formatted files, but it is inconvenient. We'll discuss an alternative way to recover these files later.

Key Files #3: Business Files

If the author was organized, they should have kept track of their expenses, income, and tax documents. You may already have had to access these documents during the probate process.

At this point, as long as you know where the files are, that's sufficient to secure them. But make sure you know where they are.

Back Up the Files

It's not enough to find the files. You also need to protect them.

Stuff happens to our devices. Fires, coffee spills, hardware defects, and so much more.

Consider purchasing a subscription to an automatic cloud backup service such as Backblaze or Carbonite. These services will back up every file on your computer to a secure server in the cloud. If something happens to your data, you can always download the backups. I personally use and recommend Backblaze.

These services differ from cloud storage providers like Google Drive and Microsoft One Drive in one key way: cloud storage services sync your files with the cloud, meaning they keep the most up-to-date version available on all devices. If you accidentally delete a file, you have no protection. As I frequently tell authors, the cloud won't save you.

An automatic backup service backs up your work on a schedule, and it is impossible to delete files from the service without intentionally doing so. It backs everything up indiscriminately; even if you delete a file from your computer, it will remain in your backups. You literally cannot screw up. If you use the service correctly, then you'll never lose any files.

If you're lucky, the author may have already used an automatic backup service. Look through their business receipts. If they did, then you'll just need to contact the provider to have the name on the account switched to yours.

The author's manuscripts, final formatted files, and business files are the Crown Jewels of the estate. You must go to extreme lengths to protect them! If you lose them, you will severely limit your earning potential.

· · ·

The Next Decision: Keep the Files Where They Are Or Move Them

If you are going to manage the estate from the author's laptop, then you can continue using it. That will keep the files undisturbed for as long as possible.

If you prefer to manage the estate from your own computer, then you'll need to move all the files to your computer. You can do this by downloading them to an external hard drive or a thumb USB drive.

Regardless of what you do, you'll have to move the files at some point. I would be cautious about deleting anything or selling the author's computer for at least two years, and even then, I'd keep it around. As you're getting the estate off the ground, you may eventually discover that you don't have all the files (even when you thought you did). If you get rid of the computer, then you could lose items forever. Be careful.

· · ·

The Author's Phone

You may be wondering why you should bother securing the author's phone. You need to secure it because of two-factor authentication.

Two-factor authentication (2FA) is a verification method used to gain access to online accounts. After entering a username and password, you have to enter a one-time passcode to get into the account.

2FA is not required at most online accounts, but the author might have used it. And most places will send that passcode to the author's phone (unless the author was tech-savvy and selected another option).

If you sold the author's phone or terminated their phone line, you may be forever locked out of some of their accounts, and there may be nothing you can do about it. That's why it's critical to secure the author's phone. You'll be able to dispose of it safely later once you reroute all of the two-factor authentication sites to your phone number.

INVENTORYING THE AUTHOR'S WORKS

Once you've found the author's key files, the next step is to create an inventory of everything the author wrote. This will show you what the estate has. Otherwise, you won't know what needs to be managed.

You may have already had to create an inventory during probate. Or the author may already have created one for you. Don't start from scratch unless you have to.

In case you have nothing, I have created an inventory template for you. Download it at www. authorlevelup.com/heirinventorytemplate.

There are about 30 fields on this spreadsheet, but it's not difficult to fill out. I recorded a quick video that will teach you how to fill it out for each book. Plan on it taking about five to ten minutes per book. Watch the video at www. authorlevelup.com/heirinventoryvideo.

If you were an author, I would have you fill out around 100 fields, but I've streamlined this spreadsheet to keep it simple for you. It only contains the fields you will definitely need to manage the estate. If there's something else you need, you can always add it to the spreadsheet later.

(Frankly, the author should have already done this for you, so I hope that you don't have to go through my spreadsheet. If the author already did this for you, thank them. They just saved you more work than you can imagine.)

Set aside an afternoon and fill out the inventory sheet. The good news is that you only have to do this once, and once you've done it, you won't have to do it again. This inventory will become the command center for the estate. You'll know what you have, where the gaps are, and most importantly, where the opportunities are.

Here are descriptions of the fields on the spreadsheet and why they are important.

Series Name and Number. You need to know how many books are in a given series and which book readers should start with. The first book will be the entry point into the series and where you will spend most of your time if you need to make adjustments to the series.

Title, Subtitle, and Previous Titles. The title and subtitle are self-explanatory, but sometimes authors republish their books with new titles. If you know of a previous title, make sure you capture it. It'll reduce confusion later on if you happen to come across an old version of the book. If you don't know if a previous title exists, leave the field blank.

Author Name. Sometimes authors publish books under multiple pen names. If that's the case with your author, you'll want to keep this straight.

Genre and Subgenre. Knowing the genres of the book is important because it'll give you an idea of where they fit in the market and what types of readers are buying them. If you don't have a good understanding of genres, that's okay. Make your best guess based on the book cover and book description.

Publishing Style. You need to know if the book is self-published or traditionally published for reasons we've discussed previously.

Publisher. If the book is traditionally published, list the publisher. If the author used their own publishing company, list it. If the author does not have a publishing company, you can delete this column.

Formats Published. It's important to know which formats the book is published in. For example, if your author only published e-books, then getting the books into paperback is a good opportunity for you to grow the estate. If the author never published hardcover editions or audiobooks, that's another opportunity to grow your income.

Prices. Knowing the price of the books is important because you may need to change them in the future.

If you run a promotion, you'll need to change the price to $0.99, so you'll want to record what the original price should be so that you don't mess that up when it's time to return the book to full price. Also, if the author was disorganized, you may spot inconsistencies with pricing that need to be addressed.

Original Publication Date. Important to know for many reasons.

Rights Reversion Date. This is the date that you can get the rights back from a traditional publisher if the author signed a bad contract. The contract may indicate the terms of getting the rights back. Additionally, if you live in the United States, you can get the rights back 35 years after signing the contract.

Paperback Page Count. You'd be surprised how often you need the page count of the book. Just record it for future's sake.

Audiobook Details. Audiobooks are an important topic for you to track and be aware of. As I mentioned in a previous chapter, Audible is the biggest audiobook player in the market, and it forces authors into seven-year exclusivity contracts by offering higher sales commissions. When an author goes "exclusive" to Audible, it means that Audible is the only audiobook retailer that can carry the book for seven years. But that's not all. Audible also allows authors to hire professional narrators on a "royalty-share" basis, which means that the narrator will record the book for free in exchange for 50 percent of the royalties from the book in perpetuity.

If the author signed an exclusive royalty-share deal, then you need to know that for two reasons:

- You cannot do anything with the audiobook. It must remain exclusive to Audible.
- You can buy out the narrator to end the royalty-share deal so that you can expand the distribution for the book.

Should you buy out the narrator? That's your choice. It depends on your circumstances, if the narrator is willing to negotiate, and if you want to grow the estate's audiobook sales. The sales from the audio edition may or may not warrant it. It's something you need to be aware of.

If the author selected exclusive distribution but did not select a royalty-share, that means they paid the narrator up front, and you can escape the seven-year exclusivity term. You'll need to read the Audible production agreement to determine how.

If the author selected non-exclusive distribution, this means that they paid the narrator up front and are not restricted by Audible in any way. This is what you want to see! However, many authors signed exclusivity deals with Audible and the trend continues because they're the biggest player in the market.

For this reason, I've included the publication date, narrator's name, hours and minutes of the audiobook, the license (exclusive or non-exclusive), royalty-share, and the date the Audible exclusivity ends as fields on the spreadsheet. Knowing this information will help you understand your rights and avoid getting the estate into legal trouble with Audible.

Copyright Registration. If the author registered their copyright with the United States Copyright Office, you need to know that. Remember, if someone infringes on the author's works, you can't sue for copyright infringement unless the work is registered. As a general rule, most authors do not register their copyrights, but it's worth checking anyway because some do.

If you and the author live outside the United States, you can disregard this section unless you're certain that the author registered the work in the United States. Registration is not necessary for non-US citizens unless they plan to enforce their copyrights in the US.

Website Link. Include the link to the book on the author's website. This is where you'll want to send readers when you're marketing the work. If the author did their job correctly, the book page on their website should contain links to retailers where the book can be purchased.

. . .

Review The Author's Manuscript Files For Posthumous Works

Once you've filled out the inventory with the author's published works, review the author's manuscript folders and look for any unpublished works.

Hopefully, the author discussed their final wishes with you. Did they give you permission to publish posthumous works? Are there unfinished novels that you could hire someone to finish and then publish to increase income to the estate? Again, this is something the author should have discussed with you. If they didn't want posthumous works released, then obey their wishes. But if they did, you should inventory candidates.

Was the author working on a book when they died? If so, that's an easy first candidate.

Look for Short Works Too

. . .

Finally, don't forget about the author's short stories, poems, or magazine articles. You should inventory those too. I included a tab on the spreadsheet to help you capture those.

If you know that a story, poem, or article was published in a reputable magazine, make sure you capture the name of the magazine and the date published. Short stories can be streams of income for the estate too. If the author published a story in a magazine, then you can send it to other magazines to see if other magazines want to buy it. Or, you might be able to find a magazine that is willing to produce an audio edition of the story. Don't overlook the power of short works!

The Power of the Inventory

You'll find yourself referring to the inventory a lot. It'll be your command center and the holder of everything you need to know about the author's books. You can expand it over time.

If the author didn't make an inventory for you, please take the time to do this. You'll thank me down the road.

USERNAMES AND PASSWORDS

This is perhaps the most important part of securing the estate. If you cannot access the author's online accounts, you cannot manage the estate.

I hope the author left links, usernames, and passwords. If not, I'm very sorry for the predicament they have left you in.

The first account you should secure is the author's email account.

How many email accounts did the author have? The average person has two email accounts, but the author might have had more.

Start with the author's primary email address and log in to secure it. You'll need it because that's where all notifications will go. If you don't have access to a password, you can use the reset password function, which will generate an email.

Once you've secured the email address, go to the author's preferred browser. If the author was somewhat organized, you should see the links they used every day. Start by logging in to those websites and secure as many of them as you can. If you can't log in somewhere, use the password reset feature.

As you log in to some accounts, you may be asked for two-factor authentication. As you encounter 2FA, reset the phone number on the account to yours. Some 2FA is email-based; change it accordingly.

If an account offers backup codes to help you gain entry into the account, record those in a safe place.

Once you've made it through the bookmarks, you will have secured most if not all of the author's important websites needed to run the estate. As you encounter new websites, secure them.

If the author wasn't organized and didn't use bookmarks, then you have a lot more work ahead of you. I will mention some sites throughout this book; those are good starting points to find accounts. You'll need to go through the author's browser history to see what sites they visited. I would also recommend reviewing their last years' worth of credit card statements to see what services they were paying for—that will lead you to important online accounts. But hopefully, you won't have to do that.

Once You're In

Review the account's terms of service to determine if you're allowed to access the account. Some terms of service explicitly state that the account terminates upon the death of the original owner, but most do not.

Assuming the terms allow you to continue using the account, you should consider notifying the company of the author's death so that you can have the account name transferred to your name. This way, the account won't be flagged in the future. But again, read the terms of service to determine if you can do this. Notifying the company may also create unintended consequences and result in temporary loss of access to the account while they verify the death of the author. Be prepared for that.

Also, determine if an account is needed. Authors use many services that may not be needed after their death. Review the site to determine if it is something that may be needed in the management of the estate. Essential services include:

- book retailer accounts
- website domains
- email accounts
- sites that allow you to hire freelancers
- accounting websites
- cloud storage websites
- advertising websites
- and more.

You don't have to decide whether the account should be deleted at this point. Read the rest of this book, and then when you have a better idea of how the estate should be managed, you'll be in a better position to stop subscriptions and delete accounts. Otherwise, if you make hasty decisions now, you could create more work for yourself later.

If You Can't Log In

If you can't log in, you'll need to take the following steps:

- Review the account terms of service to see if the account terminates upon the author's death. If it does, there's nothing you can do. Notifying the company of the author's death will trigger the deletion of the account.
- Review the author's will for a digital assets

clause. This type of clause will give you explicit authority to access the author's online accounts. The company should honor this, but it may take them a long time, and there is no guarantee. They may even ask for a court order specifically ordering them to provide access, which is expensive and time-consuming. Digital assets provisions are still rare, but attorneys are starting to include them because they are desperately needed in today's digital age.

- Notify the company of the author's death and explain that you need access. You'll need to provide a copy of the will and legal documents that certify you as the executor. A digital assets provision will help considerably in your conversation with the company.

- Understand that companies don't have to grant you access. If a company refuses, you'll need to determine the importance of the account and discuss it with your estate attorney. There's probably no need to fight for access to an account that the author rarely used; but if it's a book retailer, that's a different story.

Consider Using a Password Manager

If you're overwhelmed with all the passwords you now have to remember, you're not alone.

According to Dashlane, a password manager company, the average person has 150 online accounts.

If you have 150 accounts and the author has 150 accounts, that's 300 accounts!

If the author was one of the millions of people who use the same password on all of their accounts, I highly recommend that you break that pattern. It may be convenient, but it is unsafe and will expose you to hacking attacks.

A few times a year, there's always a story on a major media outlet about a company whose usernames and passwords were stolen by hackers. Invariably, the users whose accounts were breached had easy-to-guess passwords, like "password" or "123456." It's funny, but people still do it even though they know the risks.

Cyber security best practices dictate that you should have a strong password that includes lower- and upper-case letters, numbers, symbols, and a reasonable character length, usually no less than 10 characters.

But you're probably thinking, "I can't remember passwords if I use a different one on every site!" And you're correct.

Your first inclination might be, as many do, to write your usernames and passwords down in a notebook that you keep on your desk, but that's inconvenient. It's also not secure if your home is burglarized. If your home burns down or is lost in a catastrophe such as a tornado or a flood, you'll lose all your passwords.

So what do we do?

I strongly recommend a password manager. A password manager is a secure digital vault that helps you to safely and conveniently store all of your login credentials. It also automatically fills in your username and passwords for you. Popular password managers include 1Password, LastPass, Dashlane, and Bitwarden.

Here's how you enter a password without a password manager:

- Go to the website and click Log in.
- Remember the username and password.
- If you can't remember the password, consult your notebook or a digital file that has all your passwords, which takes time.
- Enter your username and password correctly.
- If you don't remember the username or password, you have to click the "Forgot Username or Password" button and follow the steps, which is a hassle.

Here's how logging in with a password manager works:

- Go to the website and click Log in.
- Your password manager autofills your username and password.
- You're in.

If you ever change your username or password, the manager will update it automatically. If you create a new account, the password manager will store it for the next time you need to log in.

(And yes, I recognize that browsers can store your login information, but they're not secure. If someone gets access to your Google account, for example, they will also inherit your passwords if you use Chrome. It's not safe!)

Password managers also sync between your devices, so you have access to your passwords no matter what device you are on. Major password managers can be used with any operating system and any browser.

They are reasonably priced too. I pay around $40 per year for 1Password.

I use 1Password to generate very long, difficult passwords, and I keep them in my vault. I have a master password that gets me into the vault. I only have to remember one password, and it has been ages since I have had to click that "Forgot Password" button. I can't tell you how much time I have saved over the years NOT having to remember passwords.

Perhaps the best security feature that password managers offer is emergency access. With this feature, you grant emergency access to a designated person. For example, if I happen to get locked out of my account, I can use a trusted contact who will get instant access to the vault so I can reset my master password. You can use this feature with your heirs; if you designate an heir to have instant access to your account if you die unexpectedly, they can get in immediately and recover all of your passwords!

With a password manager, I enjoy secure passwords, the convenience of being able to autofill them in my desktop and phone browsers, and the peace of mind that my heirs will have access to everything.

If you have concerns about storing all of your passwords in one place, you are justified. After all, if someone gets your master password, then they have all of your passwords. However, you can secure your password manager with two-factor authentication so that if someone guesses your master password, they still can't get into your account.

My opinion is that the convenience and security of a password manager are superior to using one password on all of your sites (or writing them down on paper). Even if someone were to guess your master password, they still can't get into your account if you use two-factor authentication correctly.

If you are using the same password everywhere, if someone guesses one password, they now have them all. You probably won't have a clue that a breach happened, or which of your accounts are vulnerable. Operating without a password manager is far riskier in my opinion.

At least with a password manager, if one of your accounts is hacked, your liability is limited to that password. You can generate a new one to secure your account, and you'll know that your other accounts are safe because they all have different passwords.

If you're still leery about the security of a password manager and won't take my word for it, then consider that many IT and cybersecurity professionals strongly recommend them too. Do some research on them and check them out for yourself.

I recommend 1Password or LastPass. I have used and enjoyed both services. 1Password has a better track record of security and more features. LastPass has had some security vulnerabilities in recent years, and many people are moving away from it, but it's still a very good password manager.

In any case, whether you use a password manager or not, you still need to store your passwords in a place where your heirs can find them. (Yes, I said your heirs. You have to plan your estate too!)

The requirements for correctly granting access to your passwords for your heirs include:

- Gathering all of your passwords
- Keeping them up to date
- Keeping them in a place your heirs can find them

Using a password manager accomplishes all of these goals with little to no effort.

If you use pen and paper or another way, you'll have to be creative. If you write your passwords down, you have to be very, very careful to update your notebook any time you change a password. Failing to do so could be catastrophic.

Update Credit Cards and Bank Accounts

. . .

If the author pays for a service that the estate needs, update the credit card on file.

If the account pays the author, make sure you update the bank account on file once the account is changed to your name.

When the author passed away, their bank account was likely frozen unless they were organized. Eventually, the bank account would have been closed during probate. If that happened, I have no idea how long it has been since their passing, and they might have money due to them. Be sure to watch out for that.

Hopefully, you will be able to capture all the credit cards and bank accounts, but you may not; this is another reason why the author's email accounts are so important. If there's a problem, you'll receive an email.

EMAIL ACCOUNTS

Let's spend some more time on email accounts.

You should have been able to find the author's primary account, but they probably had a few more email accounts.

Many authors use one email account for personal affairs and another for writing affairs. I'll give you my email setup as an example.

I have:

- a personal email.
- a "professional" email for my insurance

career; I use it when applying for jobs, corresponding with recruiters, and so on.

- a "burner" email address that I use for sites where I don't want to give my preferred email address.
- a separate email for my YouTube channel so I can manage those emails cleanly.
- and more.

But that's not all. I also have email addresses associated with my website. I also have:

- A "domain" email address that I use mainly to improve my email marketing deliverability.
- A "contact" email address that I use for contact forms. I have hired VAs to help manage my emails in the past, and I believe giving them a dedicated email address looks more professional to readers.

To review, that's at least seven email addresses I have to manage. If you don't understand how website email addresses work just yet, don't worry —we'll cover that when we get to the website chapter.

To make matters worse, I haven't always been consistent with which email address I use to sign up for accounts, magnifying the problem even more.

I hope the author wasn't anything like me, but chances are they probably were!

Finding and Streamlining Email Accounts

Once you've identified all the author's email accounts, you should determine what they are used for and what types of emails arrive in each. By this point, you should have a good idea of all the usernames and passwords the author used in their publishing business and which emails were used to sign up. You should have been able to change the email address on record to your own.

If you've done that and are confident that there are no other accounts out there, then you can leave the email addresses alone. I wouldn't delete them, but I'd leave them alone and monitor them regularly. You never know what will arrive in the author's inboxes.

Let me repeat that: you never know what will arrive in the author's email inboxes!

Some examples:

- a fan sends a heart-felt email.
- you learn about an account that you didn't know existed.
- you receive a notice of copyright infringement that the author committed while they were alive.
- you receive a letter from a rights buyer wanting to license the books into a particular format.

I can't say this enough: you never know what types of emails could arrive, so make sure you monitor the author's email inboxes!

You can monitor the email accounts in one of two ways:

- you can set up an email forward so that any emails that arrive in the author's email inboxes will be routed to your email address.
- you can add the author's email inbox to your email service provider such as Outlook so that you can check their inbox at any time.

If you don't know how to do these things, just do an internet search for "set up email forwarder for [insert name of email service]" or "add email accounts to [insert name of your email provider app]". They're not hard to set up.

. . .

Develop an Email Strategy

Once you've secured all the email accounts, next you need to decide on the flow of future emails.

What will be the primary address that the estate uses to receive emails? It may require you to set up a new email address.

The author will also have a contact form on their website—I highly recommend that you keep this operational, so you'll want to remember that moving forward. We'll talk about contact forms later in the book. They're a phenomenal source of opportunities for the estate.

By determining an email strategy, you'll put a professional face on the estate whenever you must perform business dealings.

.

ORGANIZING THE ESTATE: APPLYING THE PIECES

Now that you've secured the estate, it's time to discuss how all the pieces work together. When you understand the nature of each piece, you'll be able to make informed decisions on how to manage the estate.

THE AUTHOR'S DOMAINS AND WEBSITES

Almost all authors have a website. A website is the author's home base; it's where readers go to learn more about the author and their books. Its importance cannot be understated, and it should be the home base of the estate as well.

If you didn't secure the author's website in the previous section, this section will give you the knowledge to do so.

Website Basics

. . .

Websites receive traffic from two key sources.

The first and most significant source of the traffic to an author's website is from readers. The best practice is to include a website link in the back of the book as advertising for readers who finish a book and want more from the author. This drives readers to the author's website, where the author can sell more books to them.

The second source of traffic is from general website searches. If the author was featured on a blog, magazine, or YouTube video, then people will search for the author.

You never know when or how someone will find their way to the author's website, so it is imperative to keep the site operational.

Whatever you do, do not let the website lapse. The author paid for their website services on an annual basis, and you will have to keep making the payments. If you stop paying, then the author's website will disappear, and it will be devastating to the estate because you won't be able to get it back.

Always keep the payments up to date and never, ever let the website expire!

I believe it's best to think about the author's website and domain like a piece of real estate. Just like you'd maintain a home to pass down to your heirs, you also want to make investments and updates to the author's website so that it grows in value over time.

You don't have to actively update the website all the time, but you do want to keep it up to date. And keep those hosting bills paid!

Understanding the Website

When you buy a website, the first thing you buy is a domain.

Simply put, a domain is the name of a website. One of my domains is authorlevelup.com. You have to choose a domain that no one else is using, and you must pay an annual fee to keep it. If you don't, the name will lapse and someone else can buy it.

Domains are incredibly valuable. Some of the most popular websites on the internet are domain names that were purchased in the nineties when few truly understood how valuable they would be. Think aa.com for American Airlines or Cars.com.

Domains are so valuable that companies will pay big money to acquire a domain name from an existing owner. At the time of this writing, the most expensive domain ever purchased is carinsurance.com, for which the current owner paid $872 million!

The term domain is also loosely used to describe the entire property that your website rests on. When you purchase a domain, you also purchase a website hosting package and the rights to access a back-end dashboard to create and administer your website. When I use the term domain from now on, I'm referring to both your domain name and your website.

When you purchase the rights to a domain name, you register it with a website hosting provider. These providers include Bluehost, GoDaddy, HostGator, DreamHost, and Namecheap, to name a few. Your hosting plan includes the ability to install a website. It also includes domain-specific email addresses that you can use for branding purposes.

For simplicity's sake, a website contains a front-end and a back-end.

The front-end of a website is what you see when you visit it in a browser.

The back-end is the system you use to make changes to the front-end. This is also known as a content management system (CMS). For most authors, this back-end is WordPress, which is the most common CMS. Others include Squarespace and Wix.

If you've never managed a website before, then you should watch some YouTube videos on the topic. Figure out which hosting provider the author used and learn how to access their website back-end.

Fortunately, running a website isn't too difficult; you just have to learn how.

If the author has domain-specific email addresses, you'll find them on the website hosting provider's dashboard too. An example of a domain-specific email is author@authorname.com.

It should also be noted that there are generally three different logins you'll need to secure:

- the author's back-end
- the author's account at the hosting provider
- the author's domain-specific email addresses

Each of these will have a different link, username, and password. Make sure you can access all three.

The Anatomy of an Author Website

An author website has several fundamental pages.

The home page is the first page that readers visit. Most authors will include a link to their latest book, a request to sign up for their email newsletter, and special news. In the case of the estate, a home page should have the author's most popular titles (or, if the estate publishes titles, those too).

A newsletter signup is a form that readers put their email address into to receive updates from the author. We'll talk about email marketing later in the book, but this can be helpful for the estate to communicate with existing fans.

The second-most visited page on any website is the about page. The about page contains biographical information about the author and what they're about. It's the perfect place for the estate to pay tribute to the deceased author.

The third-most visited pages on any author website, and perhaps the most important, are the book pages. Most authors set their websites up so that every book has a dedicated page. For example, one of my book pages is www.michaellaronn.com/dreamborn.

A book page contains the following elements:

- The book title, subtitle, series, and series number

- The book cover
- The book description
- Links to where readers can buy the books

Some book pages contain additional content such as reviews, testimonials, samples of the book, and more.

The most important thing about book pages is to make sure that the links on the pages are always valid. WordPress needs to be updated regularly (which is an automated feature), but for some reason, sometimes links are broken after an update. I don't know if this is the case with other CMS platforms, but as an author, my biggest struggle with my website is policing links.

The final website page we need to discuss is the contact form. This is where readers can ask the author questions. Now that the author is deceased, the contact form is where readers can ask the estate questions.

You might be thinking, "But I don't want to answer questions." That's understandable. However, you should keep the contact form open because it's where opportunities will come from. If someone wants to license the rights to one of the author's books, the contact form is how they're going to communicate with you.

Besides, you may enjoy receiving fan-mail too! Consider putting together a page on the author's site that answers the most common email questions the author receives and direct readers to the right places. I suspect that if readers know the author is deceased, they're not going to bother the estate that much. As an author, I receive a lot of fan-mail, but I don't expect that to be true when I'm gone.

Now that you understand the key elements of an author website, take some time to review the website you've inherited. How is it set up?

Are there pages that can be retired? For example, on my website, I have a page that promotes me as a public speaker. When I'm gone, that page won't be needed anymore.

Are there pages that need to be modified?

Are there pages that need to be added?

The website is your property now.

Managing the Author Website

The good news is that you won't have to spend nearly as much time as the author did in maintaining the website. You're unlikely to have news very much unless you are actively publishing titles.

As you get familiar with the website, what you should do is figure out what work needs to be done. You can learn how to do it yourself or you can find one of the author's friends to help you. Or, you can hire a freelancer on a site like Upwork for a small fee, tell them what needs to be done, and then grant them access to the CMS so they can make the changes for you.

In any case, my laundry list of to-do items for a deceased author's website would be the following:

- Update the website CMS software to the latest version.
- Review the website for any broken links and correct them accordingly.
- Ensure that all the author's books are represented on the site.
- Remove any obsolete material.
- Ensure the contact form works.

Once you've done these things, then the website should be self-sufficient. You'll just need to review it a few times a year to ensure the CMS is up to date and that there are no new bugs on the website.

Once or twice a decade (maybe more), you'll need to hire someone to refresh the website design to keep it modern and up to new web standards. This will cost you, but it will keep the website relevant for future readers.

Remember, the website is the estate's home base.

ONLINE ACCOUNTS WITH BOOK RETAILERS

The book retailer websites where the author did business are the places that will pay you every month.

By now, you should have secured all of the author's retailer accounts. This chapter will help you understand these websites better.

Retailers and Distributors

A book retailer is an online store that sells the author's books. Amazon, Apple, Barnes & Noble,

Google Play, and Kobo are the most popular book retailers at the time of this writing.

Retailers carry e-book, print, and audiobook titles, but not necessarily all of them. Amazon carries everything, but Google only sells e-book and audiobook titles, for example.

The best practice for self-published authors is to publish directly with a retailer whenever possible. This is because retailers usually offer user-friendly dashboards that make uploading books easy, and they pay a higher commission if you sell through them directly versus through a book distributor (which we'll cover next).

If the author has accounts directly with retailers, then you know that the author published directly with those retailers.

While authors prefer to publish directly with retailers, this is not possible with every retailer. Smaller retailers have a storefront but not a dashboard for authors. They want self-published books but don't offer the ability for authors to publish directly with them because it's too expensive.

That's where distributors (also known as aggregators) come in. A distributor is a third party who takes an author's book and distributes it to places that the author can't get into by themselves.

At the time of this writing, the most popular distributors for e-books are Draft2Digital, PublishDrive, and StreetLib. The author creates an account at the distributor, uploads their books, and the distributor delivers the e-book to retailers around the world that the author wouldn't have been able to reach otherwise. The distributor takes a ten percent commission on each sale.

There are print distributors as well. IngramSpark is the most common. IngramSpark has a worldwide distribution network that makes it possible for bookstores to order an author's book. Note that I said "makes it possible"—it's not a guarantee. But you're much more likely to get into bookstores if you distribute through Ingram.

There are also audiobook distributors such as Findaway Voices and Author's Republic who will distribute audiobooks to audiobook retailers all over the world.

There is one quirk with distributors that you need to know about. While most people use them to get into smaller retailers that they couldn't reach otherwise, some authors use them to get into big retailers too. For example, an author could use a distributor to send their books to Apple even though Apple offers a direct dashboard. In Apple's case, for a very long time, you couldn't upload directly with them unless you were an Apple computer user. Even though that's not true anymore, some authors continue to use distributors for Apple out of habit.

In other cases, some authors prefer to use distributors to minimize the number of dashboards they have to access to. These authors feel that the ten percent commission is worth it.

I share these quirks merely so you can understand what choices your author made.

When you combine retailers and distributors, you create an international network where anyone can buy a book, anywhere in the world, at any time, as long as it is available.

When you're reviewing the author's book retailer and distributor websites, take note of how their distribution is set up.

A Quick Overview of Specific Retailers and Distributors

If there's one thing that's true about all retailers, it's that they're always changing. However, to help you understand the landscape, I'll cover the basics of how some of the key retailers are set up and what you need to know when logging in.

Amazon KDP

.   .   .

Amazon is the most prominent book retailer in the world. Their self-publishing service is called Kindle Direct Publishing (known as KDP).

What you may not know about Amazon is that it has stores all over the world. Each store has a unique domain. When you sell a book in a country outside your own, the sale technically is made in that country's Amazon store. Amazon converts international sales to your home currency each month before paying you.

If you see several Amazon KDP deposits in your bank account each month, this is why. For example, you could receive a payment from Amazon US, UK, Italy, Australia, and more. Amazon is the only company in this chapter that does this. All others make only one deposit into your bank account.

Amazon KDP also has a program called KDP Select. This is an exclusivity program where the author agrees to only carry the e-book edition on Amazon in exchange for increased visibility and better marketing opportunities. Amazon-exclusive books are available in Kindle Unlimited, which is an all-you-can-read subscription service that pays authors by the number of pages readers read each month. Some authors have made their entire careers being exclusive to Amazon, and it can be quite lucrative.

(KDP Select only applies to e-books, not paperbacks or audiobooks. This means that the e-book can be exclusive to Amazon but the other editions don't have to be.)

KDP also has KDP Print (formerly known as CreateSpace), which is Amazon's print on-demand company. KDP Print ships paperbacks to readers on your behalf so that you never have to keep inventory. You can also order copies of the book at cost, which means you pay the printing cost plus shipping.

When you are paid each month from KDP, your e-book, print, and Kindle Unlimited sales are rolled up together. Amazon sales reports break them out for you if you want more details.

Amazon Associates

. . .

Why is Amazon in this chapter twice? Because it has another stream of income that the author likely benefited from: Amazon Associates.

Amazon Associates is known as an "affiliate" program. In an affiliate program, a company relies on people (known as "affiliates") to spread the word about its products. In the author's case, they receive a unique affiliate code from Amazon (known as a "tag"). Any time they promote a product on Amazon, they use a special link with their tag in it, and any time someone clicks on that link and purchases a product (any product) on Amazon, the author receives an affiliate commission.

For example, if I send you an affiliate link to one of my books, and you buy it, I receive around four percent commission on that sale. For a $4.99 e-book, that's around $0.20. However, I also receive commissions on anything else you buy within a certain period. So, if you buy my e-book and then purchase a big-screen TV, I get a commission on the TV too!

See why affiliate income is so cool? It's like playing the lottery, except you don't have to pay for a ticket.

Amazon isn't the only company that offers this payment feature, but your author was more than likely using Amazon Associates. As such, this is another payment stream you will probably see reflected in the bank account. Because Amazon Associates is a different legal entity than KDP, it counts as another stream of income.

Amazon Associates also has a separate dashboard, but it uses the author's Amazon username and password. You may want to see if the author had an Amazon Associates account.

Amazon Associates is international. However, the weird thing about Amazon Associates is that you are required to sign up for a tag at each Amazon Associates store, and you have to do it in the store's home language. So, if the author was really dedicated to affiliate income, they had to sign up in English, French, Italian, Spanish, and so on. When you're logged in to Amazon Associates, you can change stores by clicking the flag button in the top navigation.

The international component is a lot of work and effort and not all authors do it, but if your author did, then you need to know about it. Amazon Associates will send emails that require action on the account from time to time. They're also known for shutting down international affiliate tags if they don't drive enough income.

Amazon Author Central

We're not done with Amazon yet. Amazon offers a dashboard called Amazon Author Central, which lets you see some basic information about all of your books in one place.

Every author has an Amazon profile that appears on the sales page. Amazon Author Central is where you update your profile. It would be a prudent idea for you to check this out and update the profile accordingly.

You can also view reviews for all the author's books on Amazon Author Central as well as sales rankings.

Amazon Author Central is a separate website, but it is accessible using the author's Amazon username and password.

Apple Books (formerly Ibooks)

Apple Books is laid out much differently than Amazon. For starters, Apple requires authors to use its iTunes Connect platform to upload books. For a long time, iTunes Connect required a Mac to use; now anyone can use it.

Apple is much more international than Amazon, and they have a bigger reach because their iOS phones and tablets are sold all over the world.

As I mentioned previously, many authors use a distributor to reach Apple instead of uploading to them directly. If you don't see a dedicated Apple account in the author's bookmarks, then they're probably selling books on Apple through a distributor.

Audible/ACX

Audible is also owned by Amazon, but because it's a separate legal entity, we have to treat them separately.

Authors publish books through Audible on the company's website, Audible Creation Exchange (ACX). While it is a separate dashboard, it requires the author's Amazon username and password.

Audible's sales reports are a mess, so consider yourself warned before you try to make sense of them. The truth is that Audible's sales payments are about as opaque as you can get in the self-publishing space.

Audible offers a "bounty" program that pays a bonus based on how many people use one of the author's special links to join Audible for the first time. For example, Audible gives me a special link for each audiobook I create. Whenever someone clicks my link and purchases my audiobook as their very first Audible purchase, then I receive a special commission. Naturally, given that Audible is the biggest player in the audio space (at least in the United States), bounties are rare, but they are nice when you encounter them from time to time.

ACX is also a messaging platform where the author can communicate with audiobook narrators. You may receive a message from a narrator from time to time.

Barnes & Noble

Barnes & Noble (Nook Press) offers a simple and straightforward dashboard. There are no international stores to worry about as they only sell in the United States. Barnes & Noble's platform used to be known as PubIt!

The financial health of Barnes & Noble has been in question for a long time. People are always predicting that they will go bankrupt, but they've managed to stay afloat. That said, at some point, the company may not survive.

Many authors use distributors to publish on Barnes & Noble instead of publishing with them directly.

Draft2Digital

Draft2Digital is a distributor, so as with all distributors, they will provide a sales report with a breakdown of which retailers your book sold at for each month. Draft2Digital's dashboard is easy to use.

Draft2Digital also has another feature you should be aware of: Paid Collaborators. We'll talk about coauthoring later, but if the author coauthored a book with another person and used the Paid Collaborator feature, the company will split the sales for both authors and pay them. This is a much safer way of working with a coauthor. If the author did this, you'll see it reflected in the sales reports.

Draft2Digital also has a sister website called Books2Read that is accessible with the Draft2Digital username and password. Books2Read is a book discovery site that offers author profiles and "universal book links." A universal book link is a link that you give out that then tells readers where to find books on all retailers. Instead of routing them to a single retailer, the user can choose which store to buy the book from. This is very useful and likely to be a helpful tool for the estate! Universal book links are automatically created whenever an author publishes a book on Draft2Digital.

Google Play

Google Play has come a long way. When I started publishing in 2014, they closed their self-publishing platform to new authors. For years, no one could get into Google Play. Those who could lamented its terrible user interface.

Fortunately, Google Play is open for business again and its user interface is much better.

At the time of this writing, Google Play only allows for uploading e-books, but you can distribute audiobooks to the Google Play store with an audiobook distributor.

IngramSpark

IngramSpark has a straightforward user interface and sales report, but there's one thing you need to know about them.

When you sell books through Ingram, you have the option of enabling "returns." When a bookstore orders books but can't sell them, they will return the book. The book will either be returned to the author or destroyed (also known as "pulped"). In either case, you'll have to pay for the returns, and these can be costly. If the author published on IngramSpark, I would watch this very closely for a few months to get a sense of how much returns are costing.

You can turn off returns at any time, but it will make bookstores less likely to purchase books from you.

If any of this doesn't make sense, I recommend researching this topic further. If necessary, contact IngramSpark to figure out the best option for you.

Kobo

Kobo is a standard book retailer that has a great reputation in the publishing community. Its dashboard is called Kobo Writing Life.

In addition to selling e-books, Kobo also has a subscription service called Kobo Plus that pays based on how much time it takes to read a book. Kobo makes one deposit each month, but it provides two different sales reports—one for e-books and one for Kobo Plus.

All Others

. . .

There are many other retailer dashboards out there, but this chapter covers the key differences.

Some smaller retailers only pay via PayPal, so that's something else to be aware of.

Most retailers offer a simple user dashboard that will be intuitive to you after you've familiarized yourself with the retailers I discussed in this chapter. Once you learn how to use one dashboard, the others are just a variation on the same theme.

A Checklist for Retailer Websites

First, make sure that you settle account ownership with all retailers and distributors. You don't want to run afoul of their guidelines.

Second, make sure the bank information at every account is updated. Most places pay monthly, so you don't want to miss out on income. Other places only pay once your account exceeds a certain threshold, such as $50 US.

Finally, make sure that you update your tax information at all the retailers and distributors you sell books at.

Making Changes to Books or Uploading New Ones

If you need to make a change to an existing book, please note that you will need to make that change at every retailer and distributor that carries the book, which means you'll have to do a lot of logging in to dashboards.

If you need to upload a new book, you'll need to upload it to every dashboard too.

If you need help on how to do any of these things, look for tutorial videos on YouTube. Fortunately, making updates and uploading new titles is not hard, but it is different for each retailer.

.   .   .

Direct Sales

In addition to selling at retailers and distributors, many authors also sell their books directly to readers using their own storefront on their websites, therefore cutting out retailers and distributors altogether.

The author will typically use a third-party website like Gumroad, Payhip, or even PayPal. These sites offer plugins that the author can use on their website to create a retailer-like experience. This is typically used for e-books and audiobooks, though it is possible with print as well (but more complicated).

When readers buy from the author's website directly, they enter their credit card information and receive the book via email. The author gets paid instantly and makes a higher commission— somewhere around 85 to 95 percent of every sale. Direct sales are amazing, but they're likely to exist in lower volume than retailer sales.

If the author has direct sales, you'll need to understand how the sales platform is integrated into the website so that you can keep it working. You'll also want to make sure you change the account name, bank account, and tax information on file too.

RECOVERING LOST BOOKS

In the Securing the Estate section, I recommended locating the manuscripts and final formatted files. These are essential items for the estate.

If you can't locate the manuscripts, I have some bad news—they may be lost forever unless you get lucky. As I said before, manuscripts are valuable because they contain drafts of the book as it evolved, research, notes, and other information that you might be able to use to your benefit.

However, if you lose the manuscript files, that's not the end of the world. You can get the final formatted files, which means that you will at least have the text of the books.

When the author published the book on retailers, they had to upload the final formatted files. If you can get the files the author uploaded, you can get the text of the books so you can make future updates. For example, Draft2Digital automatically makes these files available so you can download them at any time. If you can't find the book files, and if the author used Draft2Digital, then you have instant access to the book text. I recommend that you download the EPUB files for all the books in the author's inventory.

You can use a free app called Calibre to convert the EPUB to a Microsoft Word document. I recommend doing this and storing it along with your EPUB.

This isn't ideal, but at least it's something!

SOCIAL MEDIA

Many authors have social media accounts, and there's no doubt that social media can help grow a publishing business.

However, social media poses an interesting problem for an estate. Social media companies state in their terms of service that your account terminates upon your death. Some companies like Facebook allow people to "memorialize" their profile, but in doing that, the profile still becomes inactive.

If an author has a substantial social media following, the estate will almost certainly lose most if not all of those people. That's unfortunate because those people were probably readers.

(This is why I constantly advise people not to build their only communities on "rented" places like social media. Your audience doesn't belong to you.)

Why would an estate need to continue using social media? That's a good question. There's nothing that says that you have to use social media. If you have nothing to say and don't plan on being very active in generating new titles or refreshing old ones, then it probably doesn't make sense for the estate to have an active social media presence.

However, if you intend to be actively managing the estate, then having social media accounts in the estate's name may be important to you.

My opinion is that if the estate plans to communicate with readers on social media, then readers should know up front that the communications are coming from the estate. Otherwise, they will be confused. They're going to find out that the author died eventually. You might as well disclose it up front by including "estate" in the name of any social media accounts you create for the estate.

I can't tell you how to use social media. Everyone uses it differently and every platform is different. You'll need to research how to use a specific platform effectively. But some people are naturals at social media. If that's you, then don't discount this as a tool in managing the estate.

I believe that some readers would be interested in hearing from the estate, especially if there are posthumous titles. Social media is the only way to reach some readers. It will be a missed opportunity for many estates in my opinion.

Take stock of the author's social media presence. What platforms did they use, and did they have a substantial following? While you won't be able to communicate with those readers, it may give you an indication of which platforms are worth spending your time on.

INFLUENCER PLATFORMS

Read this chapter if the author was an influencer.

All authors are influencers to a degree, but I'm referring to influencers on blogs, YouTube, or podcasts. These require unique demands from the estate. We discussed social media in the previous chapter—that's a form of influencing too, but it's much different from what I am going to cover now.

Simply put, an influencer is someone who gathers a large following around a specific topic or idea. They make a significant amount of money from product referrals and advertising revenue.

For example, I have a YouTube channel for writers that has nearly 40,000 subscribers at the time of this writing. I review writing-related products and give opinions on the writing life. My community has come to trust my advice, so when I recommend a product or service as an affiliate, many will buy it, which compensates me financially. I also use my YouTube channel to promote new products that I create.

If the author had an influencing platform like mine, it is probably driving income to the estate.

Blogs

A blog is useful because the most popular posts are probably bringing people to the website.

If the author was a serious commercial blogger, then it's possible that every post was optimized for traffic, which means they were also optimized for income. On such a blog, you're likely to see posts promoting products, services, and even paid courses.

The best way to determine if the blog is bringing traffic is to go to Google Analytics. It contains vital statistics about the website, like how many people visit and where they come from. All authors should have an account there. (And if it wasn't in their bookmarks, rectify that. This won't be the first account that you didn't know about.)

Look for the top ten most visited pages from the last year. If any of those posts on Google Analytics are blog articles, then look at the articles and figure out what the purpose is. Maybe the author got lucky and wrote a blog post that went viral. Or maybe they really knew what they were doing. In any case, make sure the links on those pages stay active, especially if there are any book or product promotions!

There's nothing wrong with leaving a blog up, especially if it's not hurting anything. Just let it do its thing. You'll need to be careful whenever you make updates to the website, though, and take care not to break the blog in any way. A professional programmer can help you with this.

Here's an important thing to understand about blogs: if a blog exists and is driving income, don't count on that income. It may not always be there and it will probably decrease over time if the author is not actively blogging anymore.

That said, you do have some potential options if the blog was particularly lucrative.

First, you can leave it alone.

Second, you can continue it. Popular blogs have been known to continue with guest bloggers even after the original blogger is no longer blogging. This scenario will probably be unlikely for you.

Third, you can sell the blog. Don't sell the website —but the blog. You give the content to someone else in exchange for the fee and then they're free to do with it what they will. Blog articles are copyrighted works, remember. This is also unlikely for you, and it's really only applicable when the blog is a separate website from the author's works.

Fourth, you can delete the blog, but don't do that if it's driving traffic.

That's why I think you should just leave the blog alone and protect what you have. It's possible that the posts will eventually become outdated and traffic will drop. At that point, you can explore if there's anything you can do to keep the numbers up. If you determine there's nothing you can do at that point, so be it.

Podcasts

Podcasting is a popular way to grow an audience. It is a more intimate medium than blogging, and podcasters can amass a big audience.

Podcasts are similar to websites in that you have to pay for hosting. If you stop paying for hosting, then the podcast disappears. If the author developed a substantial podcast following, you'll want to consider keeping the podcast available because it could be driving people to the website.

Podcast hosting plans are based on how much audio the podcaster uploads each month. You can probably reduce the existing plan down to the lowest tier, which will save you money. For example, when I was actively podcasting, I paid around $15 per month for hosting; when I stopped podcasting, I kept the podcast available but reduced my plan to $5 per month just to keep it active.

Podcast websites also give you analytics on which episodes are the most popular. That data may be useful to you in the administration of the estate, especially if you want to keep using social media.

YouTube

YouTube channels are less common among authors, but I'll still give them a quick mention.

There are three ways to make income on YouTube.

The first is through promoting your own products or services, or the products or services you recommend as an affiliate.

The second is through YouTube's AdSense program, which requires 1,000 subscribers and 4,000 watch hours per year, which is not easy to achieve for most. AdSense pays the channel for every ad shown.

The third way is through sponsored products or brand deals, where companies will pay the creator to feature a product.

Log in to the author's YouTube channel. See how many subscribers they have and whether their videos are monetized. Look at the top-performing videos to see if any of them are wildly popular. If so, you'll definitely want to keep the videos on the channel active. Fortunately, you don't have to do anything to keep them available. I would recommend logging in at least once per quarter to YouTube so that you don't trigger any inactive account algorithms. Also, make sure that you change the bank account information on the AdSense account. You'll need to research how to do this.

EMAIL MARKETING

Email marketing is probably the best tool in the estate's arsenal to drive income.

Most authors have email lists—these lists contain the email addresses of readers who want to be notified of new releases. Authors collect these email addresses by putting a request to sign up at the back of their books. Therefore, the most devoted fans usually sign up because they've read at least one of the author's books and loved it.

By maintaining an email list of devoted fans, you can generate income without having to worry about restrictions. As we discussed in the social media chapter, the author's social media platform disappears when they die. You own your email list and no one can take it away from you.

Email List Basics

If you've never heard of an email marketing provider before, that's okay.

When you want to email someone about a new release, you cannot use a regular email provider like Gmail or Yahoo. This is against the law in many countries. Instead, you must use an email marketing provider like Mailchimp, GetResponse, or Mailerlite.

An email marketing provider offers a service that allows readers to enter their email addresses in exchange for communicating with them. They then have to verify that they give their permission by clicking a link in an email. Then, in any emails you send through the provider, the reader can unsubscribe at any time.

That's the key difference. In email marketing, readers give you permission to contact them. And they want to hear from you.

You must use an email marketing provider to stay compliant with the laws in your country and around the world. Otherwise, readers will report you, and your email accounts could be blacklisted and terminated.

There are plenty of blog articles, books, and YouTube videos on email marketing, so you can learn how it works quickly.

How to Use Email Marketing

If the author has a list of readers, you can email them to let them know:

- when books are on sale
- when a new title is out
- when an existing title has a new cover or updates

- other estate news

As I said before, I believe that the author's most devoted readers will want to hear from the estate if there is news about the author. Email marketing is the best way for you to keep the communications open.

COAUTHORED WORKS

Writing books with another person is a popular way to co-market and grow a writing platform. The author may have coauthored a book with someone else.

Coauthoring presents some unique problems with estate management.

No one should enter a coauthor agreement without a written contract. Both authors need to be on the same page.

If the author coauthored a book with another author, I hope they had a contract. If not, it will create a headache for you.

In most coauthor situations, both authors own the copyright equally. But does the coauthor agreement indicate what happens when one of the authors dies?

Both authors could decide that the deceased author's half of the copyright transfers to the other person upon one author's death. Then, when the final author dies, the rights transfer to that person's heirs. In my opinion, this is a raw deal, but there may be a good reason to do it, especially if one of the authors doesn't have any heirs to pass the work down to.

Or, the authors could decide that if one author dies, the surviving author will continue paying royalties to the deceased author's heirs. This is how I imagine most authors prefer to operate, and I will assume this arrangement for the rest of the chapter.

But you can't assume. You need to find the contract and verify.

Perhaps the most important thing to do after finding the contract is to let the surviving coauthor know about the author's passing. They may not know.

You will need to keep their contact information up to date, and they'll need your contact information too.

The next issue is payment. There are many Pandora's boxes with coauthoring that may require the advice of a lawyer. What if both authors live in different countries? What if one author gets divorced? Does the ex-spouse have a claim to royalties? Coauthoring can get complicated.

The next thing you should determine is who publishes the book. In a coauthor arrangement, one of the authors must act as the publisher. This author is responsible for uploading the book, maintaining it, and paying royalties to the coauthor.

If the author was the publisher, then you will have to assume the responsibility, which means you will be responsible for making updates to the book and paying the surviving coauthor. Tread carefully— because there's a signed contract, you can be sued if you don't uphold the author's original promise.

You also have the option of asking the other author to become the publisher if you both agree.

If you're not the publisher, then you can update the banking information with the publishing author so that the money gets deposited into the right account. Then, you need to verify that the author pays you.

Coauthoring is great for business, but the payment side is a real pain. Consider using a service like Draft2Digital's Paid Collaborator tool. With this tool, the publisher author uploads the book to Draft2Digital and adds the coauthor as a Paid Collaborator. Draft2Digital then splits the royalties.

If the coauthors didn't use Draft2Digital's Paid Collaborator feature, suggest that they do so.

Whatever you do, you'll need to communicate with the coauthor and have an open and honest conversation about the future of the coauthored book(s). The key is to get on the same page so that you and the coauthor can honor the original commitment, which will ultimately benefit both parties!

COPYRIGHT INFRINGEMENT

Copyright infringement is the unauthorized reproduction and distribution of copyrighted material. If you commit copyright infringement, you can be sued for a lot of money.

Something that should scare you is the risk that the author could have accidentally committed copyright infringement.

Here are some common ways that authors do it:

- Using song lyrics in their books. They can't do that legally without permission from the record company. Record labels can and do send cease and desist letters over this behavior.

- Quoting other copyrighted works. While this isn't usually an issue, it technically is infringement.
- Using quotes from famous people. These are also copyrighted.
- Using copyrighted images or media on their blogs or social media without permission.
- Sharing copyrighted material (such as a song) without permission.
- Not verifying the work of their cover designer. The images and fonts on a book cover are usually outsourced and copyrighted material that the designer must secure permission to use. If the designer commits an infringement, the author will be the one who gets sued.

That's just a start.

Authors with basic sense and an understanding of copyright will avoid the above items. Or they will get the necessary permission and document it.

But many authors do not understand copyright and don't learn until they make a mistake. Such a mistake can be devastating.

And yes, the estate can still be sued for copyright infringement even if the author is dead. No law prevents it, at least in the United States.

Copyright infringement can cost hundreds of thousands of dollars. In most author scenarios, the cost to secure a license is often less than one hundred dollars (like in the case of licenses on a book cover). It would be a shame to get sued for $100,000 when the author could have avoided it simply by paying for a $75 license.

Determine the Estate's Exposure

What you need to determine is whether the author covered themselves.

Your author covered themselves if:

- they refrained from using copyrighted material in their books, blogs, podcasts, or YouTube channels, or
- they used copyrighted material but secured a written license to use that material, and stored it somewhere where you were able to find it easily.

For example, I document any and all material used in my work that is not mine. I rarely quote other authors in my books; I paraphrase them instead. I never use images that are not my own.

On my book covers, I purchase the licenses to all images and fonts on the covers in case someone tries to say I committed infringement later.

On my YouTube channel, I use royalty-free music and images that are cleared for YouTube. Royalty-free means that you pay a flat fee in exchange for being able to use the image however you want without having to pay the owner a royalty.

Most importantly, I document all of this. My heirs will be able to find any and all licenses easily in the event of a dispute.

How about your author?

If they didn't cover themselves, you should fix that ASAP. Review the author's books and influencer platforms for any potentially copyrightable content that belongs to someone else. If you can't find a license to use the content in the author's records, remove the copyrighted content or see if you can purchase a license without the owner knowing about the potential infringement. It won't help you if they find out because they can still sue, but owners might be less likely to sue you if you prove that you identified the problem and rectified it without being "caught" to compel your compliance.

At the end of the day, people just want to make a living from their copyrighted content, authors included. Copyright litigation is expensive and few can afford it. But large companies don't care and will litigate just to make an example. They've got unlimited lawyers and money. That's why you have to be careful and why you need to cover your bases. You can get sued personally over something you didn't do, which should be concerning to you if the author was disorganized.

The Other Side of Infringement

You may discover that someone is infringing on the author's work.

You have a few options. First, you can ask that person to stop.

Or, you can file a Digital Millennium Copyright Act (DMCA) notice (or a similar notice based on your country). You can look up how to do this or watch videos on it.

Or, you can hire a copyright attorney to send a cease and desist letter, or, if the infringement is really bad, sue the person. However, copyright litigation is extremely expensive. I once talked to a copyright lawyer who told me that he can't try a case for less than \$100,000. Litigation is not likely to be worth your time or money.

You may choose to do nothing about the piracy or infringement. There's a school of thought in the author community that, even though infringement isn't ideal, it could potentially improve book sales. Readers who pirate work were never going to buy it anyway, and a fan is a fan, no matter how they discover the work.

Ultimately, you'll want to develop a strategy on what you will do if infringement occurs, and at what point you will take action if you feel that protecting the copyrights is worth legal action.

Beware of Committing Copyright Infringement Yourself

As the executor of the estate, you may want to release new titles or find ways to promote the author's books. You must also take care that you do not infringe on anyone else's copyright.

When publishing posthumous work, read it carefully. Secure rights to any copyrighted content or omit that content from the book.

Don't use images off the internet without permission. Instead, use a royalty-free media service like Depositphotos or Storyblocks to get the images you need.

When creating book covers, always secure licenses for all images and fonts used on the cover.

I recommend that you read some articles on how to secure permission from a copyright owner. It will serve you well in the management of the estate. Trust me when I say that copyright infringement is the last thing you want to deal with.

MANAGING THE ESTATE: MAKING MONEY

At this point, you will have secured the estate and wrangled all the pieces together. You should now have a good understanding of how the pieces are used.

Now it's time to talk about managing the estate, and how you can use all the pieces to maximize the estate's income.

AVOIDING SCAMS

Authors are magnets for scams, and the estate will be too.

There are predators out there who know that authors will do anything to realize their dreams. These predators will swindle authors out of their money and even their copyrights.

As the (probably overwhelmed) executor of the estate, you will be a prime target for bad guys. You are extremely vulnerable because:

- you are probably overwhelmed.

- you don't yet know very much about publishing.
- you control a decent number of lucrative copyrights.

This chapter is a strong warning to be careful. Scams come in all shapes and sizes.

The hallmark of a scam is that it usually comes when you're feeling your lowest. Someone will offer to make handling your estate easy and reduce the overwhelm, which is exactly what you will want to hear. Then you become a victim.

Scammers have impeccable timing. The earlier you are in your estate management journey, the more susceptible you will be.

I recommend that you follow The Alliance of Independent Authors (ALLi). This is a nonprofit organization that spotlights scams for authors. Writer Beware is another good site to follow.

Things to Watch Out For

. . .

You are in charge of the estate. **Never** give away your responsibility.

Never give anyone access to any online dashboards, no matter how tempting—a scammer can change the password, lock you out, and then steal your publishing income in seconds.

Never pay more for a service than a typical author pays. Do your research for any products or services you wish to purchase. When in doubt, get three estimates.

Never do business with anyone without researching them.

Never, ever give someone part of a book's copyright in exchange for a service. A classic example of this is giving a cover designer a percentage of the book's monthly sales. Don't do it!

Never do business with anyone without a signed contract.

Never negotiate a licensing contract without running it by an intellectual property lawyer first.

Always be suspicious any time someone approaches you with a licensing deal, especially if they're a literary agent, and especially if they are from Hollywood. They may very well be legitimate, but there are a lot of legitimately unscrupulous folks out there.

When in doubt, ask someone. Even strangers will be willing to help you if you ask. There are plenty of author communities on places like Reddit and Facebook who can answer questions you have if something doesn't feel right.

Very little in publishing gets done overnight, so if someone is putting pressure on you to make a decision, that is a red flag.

If you take at least the steps in this chapter, you'll insulate yourself from many scammers. Just be vigilant and always err on the side of caution.

LEARNING GENRES

Another important concept to understand is genre. What genres did the author write in?

Book genres are complicated and ever-morphing, but it's critical to understand where the author's books fit in the market because you can use that information to sell more books.

If you think about it, there are two main genres: fiction and nonfiction. You already know that.

It's best to think about genres granularly.

Take one of my books, Shadow Deal. It is a novel about an ex-necromancer who uses his powers for good.

The genre is fiction.

The subgenre is fantasy.

The subsubgenre is urban fantasy, which is fantasy that takes place in the modern day, usually in a major city.

If we dig deeper, the main character is a male and a necromancer.

If I wanted to market my book to readers, I would focus on the lowest levels possible: readers who like urban fantasies with male heroes, possibly necromancers.

If I marketed the book to fiction readers, that's too broad.

If I marketed the book to fantasy readers, that's better, but still too broad.

It's only when I get to the subsubgenre that I start to find the target audience, but even then, I have to go deeper.

That's how you have to think about genre.

The hardest part is perhaps finding out what genre the book is. If you've never read the author's books, how would you know?

There are a few shortcuts that can help.

First, see if the author did any market research. The best advice is to find "comparable" books in a genre and then market to readers of those books. Did the author have comparable books for each title? If so, research those books. That will give you a sense of the genre.

(However, that doesn't always work because the author may have created a mashup of different genres. But it's at least a start!)

If the author didn't do competitive research, go to the book's sales page on Amazon and look for the section called "Readers Also Bought." These are called "Also Boughts" and they're how Amazon makes recommendations to readers. In many cases, you'll see similar books to the author's.

That can give you a clue of what genre the book is in.

Another thing to know about genre is that it evolves over time. New genres are always coming into existence. The author's book may be a certain subgenre today, but it may fit better in another subgenre three years from now.

Once you find three to five comparables, write those down and check them every few years. What are the authors doing to keep the books relevant? Have the covers changed? What are the book reviews saying? Then, emulate what they are doing.

If you can find comparables, that will help you understand genre and keep an eye on changing trends.

HIRING HELP

I've mentioned several times in this book that you can hire help. The author almost certainly did.

It's impossible to do everything in a publishing business yourself. Even if you could, it would take you a long time, and the end result wouldn't be nearly as professional.

For this reason, most authors hire freelancers on a per-project basis to assist in creating their work:

- Editors help refine manuscripts.
- Cover designers create stunning covers.
- A book formatter prepares interiors for

publication. They're not needed anymore in the age of user-friendly formatting software, but you may still want to hire one.

- A web developer can help you troubleshoot problems on the author's website.
- A bookkeeper can help you keep financial records in order.
- If the estate is really making money, a virtual administrative assistant can help you with many aspects of the business.

That said, there are some things you should not hire help for. These items include any work on a retailer dashboard like uploading a book or making changes to a book's sales page. For example, we've discussed the pitfalls of giving access to your retailer dashboards.

You should also avoid hiring for work you can easily do yourself with a bit of research and know-how. For example, it's a bad idea to hire someone to help you fix a typo in a book. You can learn to do that yourself.

If you want to hire someone, first make sure the estate can afford it. If you can afford it, but you don't know whether you should hire someone, ask the author's friends, or post a question in a publishing community on social media.

If you determine that you do need to hire help, I suggest you do it. It's affordable and will save you time as long as you hire quality people and avoid scams.

The most common freelancers hired by a publishing business are editors and cover designers. There are many ways to find these individuals, but the best way is to figure out who the author used before their death. Those editors and designers are likely familiar with the author's work, and you should have a good idea of what they charge. I would start there.

You can also find freelancers using internet searches or on freelancer sites like Upwork. On these sites, you post a description of what you're looking for, and freelancers will bid on the job. You then choose the person most qualified whose bid is in your budget.

The key items to look for in an editor are experience and cost. You don't want someone who has never edited a book before. Preferably, they will have been editing manuscripts for at least a few years.

The key item to look for in a designer is whether that designer has experience in the genre you're looking to publish in. For example, it makes no sense to hire a romance-focused designer for your science fiction adventure.

I've hired many freelancers over my career, and I have a good track record of hiring quality people. If you need to hire someone, be clear in what you want, don't micromanage, and give honest feedback.

If you do it right, per-project freelancers will help you save time and create a more professional work product for the estate than if you did it yourself.

REFRESHING TITLES

Some people are surprised that a book would need to be refreshed from time to time. After all, the author already published it. What else is needed?

If the author did a good job and hired a professional editor, you will never need to change the story. Let me repeat that: don't change the narrative!

What needs to be refreshed is the book's packaging. The packaging is:

- the book cover
- the book description
- front and back matter

- the book's interior
- the price
- genre and keyword placements on book retailers

As I mentioned in a previous chapter, genres change over time. You'll need to keep the book relevant in the marketplace so it can reach new generations of readers.

The rule of thumb is to change a book's packaging every 3-5 years, or when the book's sales drop below their average for an extended period and don't seem to be coming back.

I wouldn't change the packaging for a book that is still selling well. Wait until the sales drop off. Don't fix something that's not broken. You might be able to get away with 5-7 years between title refreshes.

As a general suggestion, it's probably true that out of all the books in the estate, 20 percent of them are driving at least 80 percent of the income. (This is called the Pareto Principle. We'll talk about it again later.) If the estate has 100 books, I would suspect that 20 or so books are the biggest moneymakers. The rest probably produce smaller streams of income. If that's true, then I would put my effort into the top-performing titles first, and I would refresh those titles as sales start dropping. For everything else, you can stretch out the refreshes a little more.

If the estate has a lot of books, then refreshing titles can get expensive quickly. You don't have to follow the rule, but refresh titles as soon as you can. You can budget and plan accordingly. Maybe you only do a title or two per year. Maybe you don't do any titles some years.

Let's go through the process of refreshing a book and what you can expect.

Book Covers

. . .

The book cover is the first impression, so it's an important element to refresh. It's also an expensive mistake if you mess up.

I recommend that you hire a designer unless you are willing to learn how to design a book cover yourself. While I recommend that authors try to learn cover design, this is not practical for most executors or heirs.

Therefore, you must understand the different parts of a book cover so that you can hire a designer and communicate your intent to them effectively. Many authors struggle to articulate what should be on their cover—I want to help you avoid this mistake!

Every book cover has the same number of parts. When you understand those parts in isolation, you'll be able to articulate a better vision to your designer and increase the chances of landing a cover that improves book sales.

A book cover is a series of signals. While the art may be pretty, more important is whether the signals are speaking to your target audience.

We are going to use two working examples in this chapter:

- steampunk fantasy with dragons
- a sweet contemporary romance set in a small town

(In case you're unfamiliar with the genres I just mentioned, steampunk is a fiction genre where the story takes place in a world where steam technology is still supreme. Sweet contemporary romance is a genre of romance that takes place in the modern world and doesn't contain erotic scenes, hence why it is called "sweet.")

The Foreground

The first element is the foreground, which contains the main focal point: the characters or important symbols on the cover. This is usually what the reader sees first, so you want to make sure that the centerpiece of your cover instantly screams the book's genre and subgenre.

For our steampunk fantasy with dragons, you would want a character that says steampunk. This means historical clothes, accessories such as goggles, antiquated inventions, or even prosthetics. If the character uses magic, you want magical elements prominent. A dragon would also be helpful, either in the foreground or background.

For the sweet contemporary romance set in a small town, you would want a couple in the foreground. Clothing choices that indicate small towns might include flannel, jeans, cowboy hats, and so on. Since the story is a sweet romance, the couple's pose should be innocent. Maybe they're holding hands, or if it's a male/female story, the female is resting her head on the male's shoulder.

In the genre chapter, I had you research comparable titles to the author's books if the author didn't do that already. If you want to know what should be in the foreground, look up the comparables. What do they have in the foreground? Tell your designer to copy the look and feel of what your comparables are doing. It's that simple!

The Background

The background is everything behind the foreground, and in my opinion, it is underrated. You can put many reader signals in the cover's background.

For our steampunk example, does the story take place in a major city? The Wild West? A small town? What country? What time period? Don't underutilize your background.

For our sweet romance, we would want something that indicates a small town: a farm, a town square, a market, a rustic home, a cottage, and so on.

Don't forget to check your comps!

Title and Subtitle

. . .

The book's title is also an important signal. The font you choose and the effects on the letters are everything. At a minimum, they should match other books in your subgenre.

For our steampunk fantasy, we would want a common fantasy font with magical effects around it. We might also want it to look like steampunk, such as including gears in the typeface somehow.

For our romance, we would want a romantic font, possibly with flourishes or cursive letters.

Author Name

Don't forget about the author name. You should follow the same rules as your title and subtitle, but you'll also want to make it stand out. Your author name is a great opportunity to establish branding on your cover too.

I hope that the author established a brand look around their author name. Think about mega bestsellers like Nora Roberts, Stephen King, and

Dean Koontz. Their author names always look the same no matter what book you're looking at. This helps with name recognition.

If the author didn't establish a brand look around their name, now is the time to start. Work with a designer to establish a look, and then make sure that all titles moving forward have that look. It will cost you a little more money for the designer to create a template, but once you start moving new covers into the new look, you'll be amazed at how it will increase the professionalism of the author's book portfolio. Otherwise, if all the books look different, then readers won't recognize the author's name.

My recommendation is to put the author name in a big font at the top of the cover, but that's my opinion.

Putting It All Together

.   .   .

Let's look at the reader signals that compile our covers.

For our steampunk fantasy, we might have a cover with the following elements:

- Female heroine on the cover wearing Victorian clothing and goggles, with a prosthetic arm covered in swirling magic
- Airship and dragons in the background, flying high over the London skyline
- The book title in gold letters with embellishments that make some letters look like cogs
- The author name in a similar dramatic font

For our contemporary sweet romance, we might have a cover with the following elements:

- A couple holding hands and smiling
- A main street background, with a modern pickup truck parked on the street
- The book title in a cursive, romantic font

- The author name in big letters to establish the romance author's brand

Think of your book cover as an ecosystem. Every element has its part, but everything works together to sell your book.

This is helpful when you're ordering a cover. Break down the different elements to your cover designer and tell them what you want.

When you're working with your designer and the design doesn't look good, isolate the elements to figure out what isn't working so you can communicate that clearly to the designer.

I hope that now you'll never see book covers the same way again.

Nonfiction Book Covers

. . .

Nonfiction book covers follow the same principles and have the same parts, but you just need to review your comparables to see what they're doing. Nonfiction book cover concepts are usually simpler to convey. The covers are usually simpler too.

Book Descriptions

The book description previews what the book is about. However, contrary to popular belief, it should not tell the readers what the book is about.

The worst thing an author can do is summarize the plot. Instead, a book description needs to contain sales copy.

Sales copy is copy that inspires the reader to buy the book. It hypes the book and gets readers pumped to read it. And surprisingly, sales copy contains very little plot.

Writing sales copy is an art that would require a separate book to explain. The best way to learn what sales copy looks like is to look at your comparable books, especially the ones that have a lot of reviews. What are those authors doing in their book descriptions? Do that.

I'll also include a few book recommendations in the appendix to help you learn the basics of writing book sales copy.

Just like with book covers, book descriptions are a series of signals. We can break them down in a similar way. When you understand the components of a book description, you can write a more effective description.

Let's re-use our working examples:

- steampunk fantasy with dragons
- a sweet contemporary romance set in a small town

The Headline - Fiction

. . .

If you can only spend an hour writing a book description, spend most of it on your headline. Good headlines sell books. The best part about the headline is that if it doesn't work, you can change it —and it costs you nothing.

Here's a formula for an effective headline: character + genre signal + problem + intrigue.

With our steampunk fantasy example, here's a headline: "Luna boarded the seven o'clock train for Savannah, Georgia to visit her uncle for the summer. Too bad the train was a dragon in disguise."

With our sweet romance example, here's another: "When Pam moved back to her hometown to save her family farm, the last thing she was thinking about was love."

Be creative with your headlines, but not clever. Remember that your headline is a signal; pack as many signals to your target audience into it as you can.

.   .   .

The First Paragraph - Fiction

If the headline is the most important part of the book description, the first paragraph is the second-most important part. It serves as a follow-up to the tone and content you established in your headline.

With our steampunk fantasy example, you might talk about how Luna is an inventor whose inventions never quite work right, and how her uncle, a local businessman with no patience for science, automatically doesn't like her endeavors.

With our sweet romance example, you might talk about how Pam is a successful businesswoman returning to the town where she grew up, and all her friends were nearly as successful as her.

In any case, this is your opportunity to give the reader a first impression of your character and the story.

The Body - Fiction

. . .

I like to think about everything after the first paragraph as "everything else." It's important, but not nearly as important as the headline and first paragraph. If you don't get those two right, the rest of the book description won't matter.

To get the body right, you want to describe the stakes, the villain, or anything else that a prospective reader needs to know. The trap is summarizing your story; bestselling writers don't do that. Therefore, it pays to learn copywriting and to emulate what the bestsellers in your genre are doing.

The Call to Action - Fiction

Don't forget to end the book description with a call to action. It's just good salesmanship. Ask your readers to buy the book and find a way to make the sentence sizzle.

Nonfiction Book Descriptions

. . .

Writing a nonfiction book description is a completely different exercise. With fiction, you're creating hype; with nonfiction, you're appealing to a pain point that target readers have.

For example, for this book you're reading, the pain point I appealed to was being overwhelmed in running an author estate and having nowhere else to turn. There is a lack of resources for literary executors, so I wrote my book description from that perspective. Because I was able to speak to your pain, you bought the book. That's the difference with nonfiction.

I find that nonfiction book descriptions are much easier to write. Remember to check your comps and follow their lead.

The Front and Back Matter

. . .

The front and back matter of the book shouldn't be forgotten in a refresh.

The front matter is everything before the narrative starts. The back matter is everything after the narrative ends.

You may want to update the front matter to mention a link to the author's website. Or, you may want to update the back matter to send readers to a new book published by the estate.

At the risk of repeating myself as nauseum, check your comps and do what they're doing. The best practices of what should go in the front and back matter change over time.

Interiors

The book's interior is also something you can refresh. Again, I wouldn't change the text, but you can change the look of it. That might include updating chapter headings to include an image, changing the spacing of the text, or other visual flourishes to make the book pop.

Or, the author could have done a terrible job with the interior and you may want to refresh it. Many authors struggle with paperback formatting. Early titles may look terrible because the author didn't understand print layouts. Proper tools to do print layouts easily and cheaply didn't really exist until around 2017.

Whatever you do, remember branding: if you adopt a style, adopt that style in all books moving forward so that you can eventually bring everything into the same interior style. It will improve the estate's branding and professionalism.

Prices

You should research if you should change the price of the book. Sometimes, pricing strategies change. Maybe the author had an e-book priced at $2.99, but other comparables in the genre are getting away with $4.99. Should you change the price? Absolutely!

Or, maybe inflation has diminished the sales commissions. A $2.99 sales commission isn't what it used to be.

You should also look at series pricing. What is Book 1 in the series priced at? The sequels? Check your comps and do what they're doing! You may find that their pricing changed since you last reviewed them.

You should also take the opportunity to review the price of your book in all formats to determine if the pricing is still appropriate.

Categories and Keywords

Book retailers allow you to choose several genres that your book belongs to. Based on what you choose, this is where they will put your book on their digital bookshelves. If you choose romance, for example, they will put your book in the romance section so romance readers can find it.

Categories go a few genres deep, so it's in your best interest to find the category that most clearly describes the book. I wish it was that simple— you'll find that the available book categories don't always neatly match the content of the book, so you have to use your best judgment. If anything, just make sure that your genre selection isn't way off.

You should research which categories are available and see if the book could be put in a better category to give it more visibility. You can also ask the author's friends or an author community if you need help picking the right categories.

Categories are always changing—retailers retire old categories and add new ones regularly, so you may find that a certain category exists now that didn't exist when you last refreshed the book.

In addition to categories, retailers also give you the ability to add keywords to your book that further describe the book in the marketplace.

For a book with vampires, the keywords may be "vampires," "romance," "gothic," "urban fantasy," and "magic." That tells you a lot about what the story might be about.

I've oversimplified keywords for the sake of helping you understand the concept. Keywords require research, and they require you to understand the author's books on a basic level. Keyword research is always changing—there are always different tools and methods for doing it every few years. Search for how to do keyword research for books and that will give you the most up-to-date information when you read this.

There's some evidence that keywords are less effective than they used to be, and I think that's true. As we head into an artificial intelligence future, retailers may be able to scan books and more effectively place them in front of readers than we can with a handful of keywords. But for now, you should still learn the basics of keyword research because it doesn't seem to be going anywhere any time soon.

THE SEVEN STAGES OF PUBLISHING

Let's talk about how the author created their books. This is a simple overview but will be helpful for you to know.

When would you ever create a title? The most common titles you might want to create are posthumous works or a compilation of the author's works like a short story collection or a collection of novels. These can be great tools for the estate.

The Seven Stages of Publishing

. . .

There are seven steps to publishing a book.

First, the author must write the book. Most authors usually do this in several drafts. Others (like me) write their books in one draft. Once the author writes the book, they must edit the book, which means that they review what they wrote and make revisions until they're satisfied with the content.

Second, the author must have the book professionally edited. There are three main types of editors.

A developmental editor helps the author structure the plot and the characters. This is the most expensive type of editing.

A copyeditor edits the sentences to make sure they flow properly, and they challenge the author's word choices. This is the most common type of editing, and much more affordable than developmental editing.

A proofreader is the last line of defense. They look for typos and formatting issues that could create problems during publication. Proofreading is usually the most affordable type of editing.

If the author is traditionally published, then the publisher pays for all of the editing and solicits the author's feedback.

If the author is self-published, then the author hires professional editors themselves and works directly with them. Most self-published authors only hire copyeditors and/or proofreaders.

Third, the author must format the book for e-book and print. This is called preparing the "interior" of the book. The interior is everything between the front and back book covers.

E-books are a special file format called "electronic publication" files (EPUBs), and they require special software to create. Creating EPUBs is not complicated, and many authors use affordable software such as Vellum or Atticus to create these files.

Formatting software can also create paperback interiors, but some authors hire professional formatters because paperbacks are more difficult to create correctly.

Fourth, the author must create the book cover.

Traditional publishers handle the book cover and usually have the final say.

Self-published authors usually hire a professional cover designer. They tell the designer what the book is about and the designer creates something that looks like other books on the market. The designer will create an e-book, paperback, and even an audiobook cover.

Fifth, once the author has a finished interior and book cover, they are ready to publish the book. They upload it to places like Amazon, Google, and Barnes & Noble. Then, several hours later, readers can buy it.

Sixth, the author must "market" and "promote" the work. Marketing is just letting people who would be interested in the book know about it. Marketing is usually "passive," which means that the author does much of the work upfront. For example, every book has a "book description" that describes the book. This is a passive task; if you do it correctly the first time, then it works for you, attracting the right readers and repelling the wrong ones.

Promoting is more active, and it involves purchasing ads, doing interviews, and sharing the book on social media, just to name a few tasks.

Seventh, the author can embark on rights licensing. If they want to make an audiobook, for example, they can create that by finding a narrator to work with. Or, they can use Kickstarter to raise money to create a graphic novel. Or, they can look for a literary agent to help them license translation rights for the book in another country. At this point, the author does whatever they feel is necessary to "exploit" their copyright, which means taking advantage of their hard work. This seventh and final step is perpetual.

And then, it's time to do it all over again and write the next book!

Those are the steps the author followed to create their books. Except for the last step of rights licensing, every author follows these steps every time.

This is important for you to understand for two reasons:

- You need to know how the author created each book and who they hired.
- You may want to create a new edition of one of the author's books, or you may want to publish a book that the author wasn't able to finish.

Knowing the overall process is helpful.

LICENSING COPYRIGHT

As the executor of the estate, you may be approached to license the author's copyrights. If that happens, then you need to be ready. You may want to approach a rights buyer to start a negotiation too!

Copyright licensing must occur in writing, and that means that you will have to negotiate a contract.

Licensing opportunities come in many forms:

- movie and television deals
- audiobooks
- foreign translations

- short story or magazine opportunities to publish the author's short works
- and more

Anything can happen at any time, so it pays to educate yourself on intellectual property contracts. You can and should negotiate all contracts yourself, but when in doubt, you should contact an intellectual property lawyer for counsel. You'll pay for it, but it's better to pay a few hundred dollars for legal advice than make a mistake that could cost you everything.

And when I say a mistake could cost you everything, I'm serious. I've read and heard horror stories about authors who signed contracts with Hollywood for a movie, only to realize that they actually signed away the rights to all of their books! That's why you have to be careful.

Remember this key concept: when negotiating, limit the formats, territories, and term limits.

Formats are everything. When negotiating a contract for an audiobook, limit the contract to audiobooks only. More specifically, limit it to the specific type of audiobook needed. There are many types of audiobook formats—physical audiobook CDs, digital audiobooks, artificial intelligence audiobooks, audio dramas, and more. Carve out anything a rights buyer doesn't need. Otherwise, they can perform what's called a "rights grab," grabbing rights that you never intended.

When negotiating territories, limit the contract to the territories needed. If you're negotiating a contract for French book rights with a literary agent, why would you give away rights to all languages?

When negotiating time limits, try to limit the time as much as possible so that the rights revert to you. This way, the rights always make their way back to the estate.

Next, only negotiate the rights to the project at hand. Be very careful not to accidentally give the rights to other books away. This is why you will need an attorney's help. Sometimes contract clauses have unintended consequences and it's your job to protect the estate from those.

Another common adage in contract negotiations is to treat every contract clause as if it will be weaponized against you. If you read a contract from that perspective, it will help you ask the right questions and avoid the worst-case scenarios.

Licensing can be the biggest stream of income to the estate, so if you're not comfortable with contracts or negotiation, do some research. Licensing represents the biggest opportunity an estate can have to make income and preserve the author's legacy for generations to come.

FILLING IN GAPS IN THE CATALOG

If you took the time to create an inventory, you might have noticed gaps in the author's catalog.

For example, Book 5 in the series isn't available in paperback when all the other books are. Why?

Or, the author only produced audiobook editions for certain series but not others.

Or, certain titles aren't available widely across all distributors.

These are the kinds of issues you want to be on the lookout for.

There may be good reasons why the author left gaps. For example, my first two novels are interactive—they emulate **Choose Your Own Adventure** novels, and they are thousands of pages long. Their unique format means they can only exist as e-books—it would be impossible to produce paperback or audiobook editions. That might not be immediately obvious if I didn't explain that to my heir.

In my nonfiction series for writers, I am in the process of publishing as many books in hardcover as possible. However, print on-demand providers don't allow hardcover books beyond a certain length. My longest books can't become hardcovers for that reason. But that might be different when my heirs take over my estate!

You should learn to think about catalog gaps as opportunities. Maybe the author had a good reason for not filling that gap, but maybe it's an opportunity for the estate now.

Let me give you another hypothetical example of how I would approach this.

Let's say that the author has a bestselling series that readers love. You come up with the idea to bundle the first three books into a compilation and offer it at a slight discount as a way to introduce new readers to the series. To sweeten the deal, you include a never-before-published short story that the author wrote in the world. You design a new cover, a new interior, and a new book description. You publish the book and then you notify the author's email list with a message that says, "For the first time ever, you can relive the experience of this series and read a never-before-released short story by the author about everyone's favorite character."

Wow! Get ready for the money to flow in, especially if you can make the book available in e-book, paperback, and audio. You could even do a limited edition of each format.

That's how you fill a gap.

Be on the lookout for them. I'll bet they exist all over the catalog.

CAPITALIZING ON NEW OPPORTUNITIES

It will also be your job to push the estate in new directions that the author wasn't able to realize in their lifetime.

In a previous chapter, I used an example comparing an author estate in the years 2000 and 2007. Both of those years couldn't be any more different. The executor in the year 2007 would have suddenly had to deal with the explosion of e-books and audiobooks, something that would have been unimaginable in 2000.

If I were an executor at the time of this writing, here are some ways I would be thinking about expanding an estate.

Direct Sales

Selling books directly on the author's website is still not mainstream. This will become more viable over time as readers get more comfortable buying books directly from their favorite authors. If the estate is not capitalizing on this opportunity, it's missing out on income.

Selling e-books and audiobooks directly on a website used to be a major pain; now it has never been easier. Direct sales for print can be done too, but that takes a lot of work.

Merchandise

. . .

Can the estate create t-shirts, mugs, or other items with quotes from the author's work? Character art? Merchandise is easy to create, easy to sell, and it can open up another income stream for the estate.

Audiobooks

Audiobooks are still expensive to create, so authors produce them sparingly. It's definitely a good idea to produce audiobook editions of the estate's most popular titles. My rule of thumb is that it costs around $200 per finished hour to land a decent narrator. For a 10-hour audiobook, that's $2,000. If the book sales can pay for a narrator in six months or less, then producing an audiobook edition may be worth it.

AI Audiobooks

.   .   .

Audiobooks are on the cusp of a revolution: AI narration. Instead of paying a narrator, you can give the book to a company that will turn your text into a realistic-sounding narration. It may sound like a crazy idea, but the technology has advanced to the point where you almost can't tell that a human is reading.

It's 2022 as I write this, and nonfiction books are almost AI narration ready. Fiction AI narration still has a long way to go.

Many believe that AI narration will not replace human narration, but rather, it will create a new space where readers will be willing to pay slightly less for an AI experience, therefore expanding the amount of money an author can make from one book. Readers who might not buy a human-narrated title will be more likely to buy an AI-narrated title.

This technology will democratize audiobook creation in the same way that the Kindle democratized e-books. You'll be able to purchase an e-book, trade paperback, hardcover, human-narrated audiobook, and an AI-narrated audiobook from the same shelf.

Oh, and did I mention the cost? You may well be able to produce an AI-narrated audiobook for a third of the cost.

If I were an estate manager, I would keep a close eye on this format.

Cryptocurrencies, Non-Fungible Tokens, and Blockchain

Cryptocurrencies and blockchain are gaining steam among regular people, and it's just a matter of time before they go mainstream in the publishing industry.

I'll assume you understand cryptocurrency. I believe an important opportunity at some point will be offering cryptocurrencies as a payment option if you sell books directly.

A blockchain is a digital record of cryptocurrency transactions that cannot be altered. The blockchain removes   intermediaries   and   provides   an indisputable trail of transactions and ownership, which has potentially transformative impacts on royalties, author payments, and copyright licensing and ownership for writers.

According to Wikipedia, a non-fungible token (NFT) is "non-interchangeable unit of data stored on a blockchain. Types of NFT data units may be associated with digital files such as photos, videos, and audio."

At the time of this writing, people are selling art and music as NFTs, but at some point, books will become mainstream NFTs. Regardless of what you think about them, I believe the technology is here to stay.

Imagine being able to sell early editions of the author's novels or compilations of an author's research as NFTs. See why I told you to safeguard those manuscript files?

Limited Editions

. . .

Never underestimate the power of limited editions. They can be powerful tools, especially if you include unreleased content.

The Metaverse

We are on the cusp of the metaverse, which will revolutionize how people connect to the internet. I don't think anyone knows what the future holds with this technology.

The metaverse will unlock many new opportunities for estates to revitalize their authors' images.

There's a lot to dislike about the metaverse, especially when you consider what kind of world it could lead to. (**Snow Crash** and **Ready Player One** tried to warn us!) But it doesn't matter whether you like it or not. It's coming, and it will bring opportunities for the estate.

.   .   .

The Future Is Yours

This chapter is just the start of the many opportunities you will have to push the estate in new directions. There are no limits!

MARKETING AND PROMOTION

In this chapter, let's talk about marketing basics. It will help you build a solid foundation. There are a lot of misconceptions about marketing.

What Is Marketing?

First, let's start with the most basic of definitions: marketing is letting people in your target audience know that your product exists. Nothing more, nothing less. Marketing is all about awareness.

Contrast that with promotion, which is a targeted act that puts your product in front of your target audience.

The difference is nuanced. With marketing, you want to focus on awareness and signaling to your target audience. With promotion, you want to focus on pushing the book.

But here's the thing: if you promote a book but the packaging doesn't speak to the book's target audience, you'll waste your money. Therefore, marketing is the more important of the two. With bad marketing, no amount of promotion in the world will sell a book.

Examples of Marketing

A book cover is a function of marketing. The cover signals the genre, subgenre, themes, and tone of the book.

A book description is also marketing. It signals the same things.

A book's price point, metadata such as keywords and categories, and even the book's downloadable sample are examples of marketing.

A website is also marketing. So are the pages in the front and back matter of the book.

All these elements signal to readers what the book is about and whether it is for them.

Examples of Promotion

Amazon advertising, Facebook advertising, and email newsletter blasts are classic examples of promotion. When using them, you are "pushing" the book to readers. Promotion is also paid, but not always.

The 80-20 Rule

. . .

There is an important rule in productivity, business, and marketing called the Pareto Principle, which states that 20 percent of the causes will drive 80 percent of the effects. To speak English, 20 percent of the activities you do every day will drive 80 percent of your sales.

Marketing is the 20 percent. Get that right, and you have an unlimited sales ceiling. Pair it with smart promotion tactics and you'll have a recipe for success.

I also like to think about marketing and promotion as an iceberg. When most people think of book promotion, they think of promotion because that's what most people see. However, to use the cliché, promotion is just the tip of the iceberg. Everyone knows that the majority of an iceberg's mass is beneath the surface. Marketing is the work you do beneath the surface. No one ever sees it, no one ever thinks about it, but it's ultimately what will make you money.

Remember the distinction between marketing and promotion. It's easy to confuse them.

. . .

Now we can talk about paid promotion strategies. If you've got a little more money and are willing to spend it, then you have more marketing options available to you. This chapter will cover them at a high level.

Email Marketing

Email is king. When I first started publishing, email lists were optional but strongly recommended; now, they're required. In today's ever-changing market, where you can lose your platform in an instant, it is smart business sense to build a list. No one can ever take your list away from you, and if something happens, you can communicate with your audience.

Use whatever service the author used. There are many other email service providers too, such as Mailchimp, SendFox, Mailerlite, Aweber, and more. They are all easy to use, though you may need to watch some tutorials to learn how to use them correctly.

I recommend emailing your list whenever the estate has important news or a new release. This may not be very often, and that's okay. Readers will understand that.

I also recommend creating an autoresponder sequence if the author did not have one already. An autoresponder is an automated email that goes to a subscriber after a certain period. When people sign up for my lists, they receive an autoresponder with a free book, and then an autoresponder once per week for around six weeks. The sequence gets them up to speed with who I am, why I write, why they should care, and what other books I have available. I affectionately call autoresponders "salespeople." If you do them right, they will literally sell books while you sleep. I swear by them. I even have an autoresponder that fires 365 days after a subscriber has been on my mailing list that sends them a coupon for purchasing any book on my website directly at a discount. You can be creative with autoresponders, and that's why I love them.

Whatever you do, develop a smart email strategy.

. . .

Book Promotion Sites

A book promotion site is a form of email marketing where you sign up for a promotion slot, and the service emails a link to your book to its mailing list subscribers. A few days before the promotion, you discount the book to $0.99 so readers can get it for cheap.

Sites such as BookBub, Book Sirens, and Book Barbarian have amassed mailing lists of tens of thousands of readers, and this is a fantastic (and cost-effective) way to promote your book. Better yet, chain book promos together so that you have multiple promos hitting over a short period. This is very good for book retailer algorithms.

There are so many book promotion sites that I hesitate to name any; they are always coming and going. Stay up to date in an author community or listen to a self-publishing podcast to find out what the most effective sites are at the time you read this.

A word of caution: just because a service has a mailing list, that doesn't mean it will be effective.

Do the best you can to target mailing list sites that have segments of readers in your genre; otherwise, you may not get the most value out of the promotion. For example, it's not a good idea to promote your science fiction book to a mailing list of mystery readers. It can hurt your book's chances. If a reader who is not in your target audience purchases the book and doesn't like it, you may receive a bad review. Be selective with book promotion sites.

Getting Reviews

Securing more reviews for a book is a great way to boost sales. Fortunately, you can give a free copy of a book to readers in exchange for an honest review. You could start with your existing list or you can use a service like Book Sirens (or a service like it). These services connect readers with free books in the genres they're interested in.

But do keep in mind one important rule: never, ever pay for reviews! It's unethical and it will get your account canceled at book retailers. Never compensate a reader for a review. The only thing you can do is give away a free copy of a book in exchange for an honest review. That's it.

Paid Advertising

I also recommend weaving in paid advertising at places like Amazon Ads, Facebook, BookBub, and even Instagram or YouTube if those suit your brand. Paid advertising is cheap right now, and it will never be this cheap again. Yes, you do have to spend some money, and you do have to learn pay-per-click advertising, which isn't the easiest thing in the world to learn. But I don't know any successful, full-time author who does not use this advertising method. If it works for them, you can make it work for you.

To have effective advertising, you must have effective packaging for the author's books, but we've covered how to do that.

I recommend investing in a paid online course to help you understand the advertising strategies for the platform you want to advertise on. I also recommend that you only start with one platform. Advertise there until you master it and are making a healthy profit. Then you can expand.

At the time of this writing, I recommend Amazon advertising as a good start. Amazon doesn't spend your money quickly (like Facebook), and it is easy to learn.

The Author's Website

The author's website is a great place to advertise books too.

You should showcase new releases and popular titles on the home page. You can also find other creative ways to showcase books on the site's most visited pages.

. . .

Marketing Wrap-Up

Marketing and advertising don't come naturally to most people, so expect a learning curve. But you can do it!

Marketing and promotion methods are always changing. I know I keep saying that, but this is especially true in marketing. What works today may not work tomorrow, so you'll need to do a lot of research to figure out what works best for you.

If you're lucky, the author left some documentation on the marketing methods that worked for them. If not, you'll have to experiment for yourself. I recommend joining an author community because authors love to share successful marketing strategies. You might be able to make friends with a few authors who can give you some tips. That's the best way to learn.

TRACKING INCOME

I recommend that you develop a system to determine how much money you are making. Since you're running a business, you'll want to know where your money is coming from.

However, an estate can have many income streams, so the process of tracking sales can be overwhelming.

You have three choices: track sales at the income level, track sales at the retailer level, or both.

If you track sales at the retailer level, then you're not really tracking them. As the money comes in, you record it and then distribute it to yourself and other heirs as necessary after any necessary publishing expenses. You'll know how much money the estate makes at each retailer and distributor, but not much more than that.

If you track sales at the book level, then that means you'll know to the penny how much book is making each month, and over time. This is harder than it sounds and requires more work because you'll have to dig through the sales reports that retailers and distributors provide. Every sales report is different. If you have many dashboards to check, then this will get overwhelming (and frustrating) very quickly.

A first option, if you're savvy with Microsoft Excel macros, is to use those to aggregate all the reports together, but that's complicated and most people don't have that skill set.

A second option is to use a sales tracker such as Scribe Count or Trackerbox. Sales trackers will track your sales across all dashboards and roll them into an easy-to-understand report. While I will confess that I don't know if these services are 100 percent compatible with all retailers' terms of service, there's no denying that this is the easiest way for heirs to understand the author's publishing business without getting too technical.

There are tradeoffs (one of them being that have to share your data), but your time is everything, and trust me when I say that calculating sales can be a time suck. If you elect to use a sales report service, make sure you review the terms, your retailer terms, and the company's security practices to determine if your data is safe with them.

I would avoid sales trackers that require retailer passwords—don't give your passwords out. New generations of sales trackers can track your sales without your passwords, which is much safer.

I wouldn't normally recommend a sales tracker for authors, but I think the convenience and time savings is worth it for an executor.

I track my sales at the income and book level. I don't use a sales tracker; instead, I invested in Microsoft Excel macros and hired a programmer to help me create a system that pulls all my sales reports together into a single spreadsheet that I can run reports from. I know exactly how much all of my books have made. If you ask me about book sales for a given title in a given month, I can get the answer for you in less than five minutes.

I don't expect you to do that, but it's definitely something to aspire to. The more sales data you have, the more you can look for opportunities. Maybe one of the author's books is suddenly selling a lot in a certain country. That could be an opportunity. Or, maybe the sales for another title have dropped off and it's time for a refresh. You won't know any of this unless you track the sales at the book level.

PREPARING THE ESTATE FOR YOUR HEIRS

I'll end with a final word of caution.

I hope the author took the time to organize their estate and make things easy for you. I really do.

If they did not, and if you want to keep the author's books alive, then it's now your responsibility to create a well-managed estate. And, if you want to ensure that the books survive you and make income for your heirs, then you will have to create a system for managing the estate that can be passed down to the next generation.

You'll need to develop a system, and you'll need to include the author estate in your own estate plans.

Even if you're in good health, be thinking about how to protect and preserve the estate if something were to happen to you. Who will take over?

If anything, this is a golden opportunity for you to correct all the sins the author made in their estate planning.

I wrote a book called **The Author Estate Handbook** that can help. It's written for authors, but now that you understand the estate, it should make sense to you. You may need to look some things up, but the book will at least point you in the right direction of what estate planning for an author should look like. It may also give you some additional ideas about how to manage the estate.

THE SAVVY ESTATE MANAGER

Let's recap everything we learned because we covered a lot!

As the author's heir, you have inherited a small business. You are now the owner of that business.

The estate makes money from copyrights. Every book is an infinite bundle of rights that you can exploit in many, many ways. Your job is to cultivate the book portfolio and find new ways to expand the copyrights.

There has never been a better time to run an estate. The digital era of self-publishing has democratized book creation. You can create, publish, and update books easily. Anything you can't do, you can hire someone to do cheaply.

As the manager of the estate, the first stage of running the estate is to secure the estate:

- You must secure all the author's devices, manuscript files, final formatted files, and business files. You'll need these to manage the estate properly.
- You should also take the time to create an inventory of all the author's works so you know what you have. The inventory will be your command center.
- You will be in charge of many online accounts that the author used to run their business. The most significant of these will be the author's email accounts and the book retailers and distributors where they sold their books.

The second stage of running the estate is organizing the estate:

- Understand the author's website and how to update it. Keep the domain operational and paid for!
- Change the name, bank accounts, and tax information on file with the author's book retailers and distributors.
- Consider creating social media accounts in the name of the estate.
- Consider incorporating email marketing into the estate by leveraging the readers that the author already has.

The third and final stage of running an estate is managing it, which is the best part.

In managing the estate, beware of scams and do everything you can to avoid them. You should also avoid copyright infringement. This is also the best time to familiarize yourself with the author's books and learn the genres the author wrote in.

It's your job to ensure that money continues flowing into the estate and that you find new income streams. You can do this through:

- refreshing the packaging of titles
- creating new titles
- licensing
- filling in gaps in the catalog
- capitalizing on new opportunities and emerging technology
- marketing and promoting the works

Whenever the estate has news or a new title to share, that's when you should notify readers. It's also a prime opportunity for marketing and promotion, which can take a long time to learn how to do correctly.

You should also track the income the estate receives so you can spot new opportunities and trends.

Don't forget to do your own estate planning! Ideally, you'll be passing this estate down to someone else, so start planning for that now.

Most importantly, take care of yourself. The author has asked a lot of you, and if you're reading this book and made it this far, it means that you're open to the work that is required. I'm confident that you can do it. It won't be easy, but I believe publishing is rewarding.

The books you are managing are helping people all over the globe in ways that you can't imagine. That's a beautiful thing.

Good luck on this journey. If you're successful, take some time and share your success with the author community. As I said before, you're a pioneer. You don't have to travel on this road alone.

I've included an appendix with some resources I mentioned in this book to help you if you need to do some additional research.

Happy estate managing!

MEET M.L. RONN

Science fiction and fantasy on the wild side!

M.L. Ronn (Michael La Ronn) is the author of many science fiction and fantasy novels including **The Good Necromancer**, **Android X**, and **The Last Dragon Lord** series.

In 2012, a life-threatening illness made him realize that storytelling was his #1 passion. He's devoted his life to writing ever since, making up whatever story makes him fall out of his chair laughing the hardest. Every day.

Learn more about Michael
www.authorlevelup.com (for writers)
www.michaellaronn.com (fiction)

MORE BOOKS BY M.L. RONN

Books for Writers

Indie Author Confidential (Series)

How to Write Your First Novel

Be a Writing Machine

Mental Models for Writers

The Indie Writer's Encyclopedia

The Indie Author Atlas

The Indie Author Bestiary

The Reader's Bill of Rights

The Self-Publishing Compendium

150 Self-Publishing Questions Answered

Authors, Steal This Book

The Indie Author Strategy Guide

How to Dictate a Book

Advanced Author Editing

Keep Your Books Selling

The Author Estate Handbook

The Author Heir Handbook

Interactive Fiction: How to Engage Readers and Push the Boundaries of Story Telling

Indie Poet Rock Star

Indie Poet Formatting

2016 Indie Author State of the Union

More Books for Writers:

www.authorlevelup.com/books

Fiction:

www.michaellaronn.com/books

APPENDIX: HELPFUL RESOURCES

If you need some primers on copyright and what you and your heirs can do with your work, check out the following resources.

The Copyright Handbook by Stephen Fishman.

"Harvard Law School's CopyrightX" series on YouTube: https://www. authorlevelup.com/Harvardcopyright

Books on Writing Sales Copy

. . .

How to Write a Sizzling Synopsis: A Step-by-Step System for Enticing Readers, Selling More Fiction, and Making Your Books Sound Good by Bryan Cohen

Gotta Read It! 5 Simple Steps to a Fiction Pitch That Sells by Libbie Hawker

How to Write Fiction Sales Copy by Dean Wesley Smith

Estate Planning

Estate Planning for Authors: Your final letter (and why you should do it now!) by M.L Buchman

Estate Planning (in Plain English) by Leonard D. DuBoff and Amanda Bryan

Plan Your Estate by Denis Clifford

More Books By M.L. Ronn on Estate Management

. . .

Keep Your Books Selling

The Author Estate Handbook

www.ingramcontent.com/pod-product-compliance
Lightning Source LLC
Chambersburg PA
CBHW022049020426

42335CB00012B/609